The Creation Care Bible Challenge

A 50 Day Bible Challenge

Forward Movement
inspire disciples. empower evangelists.

The Creation Care Bible Challenge

A 50 Day Bible Challenge

Edited by Marek P. Zabriskie

FORWARD MOVEMENT

Cincinnati, Ohio

Preface

Peak religious moments are not confined to churches. Many of us have had such moments in nature. This doesn't detract from the important role that churches play but rather reminds us that in the beauty of creation, we encounter God's cathedral in its widest sense.

Sir Francis Bacon, the sixteenth- and seventeenth-century philosopher, scientist, and advocate for the scientific method, noted, "God has, in fact, written two books, not just one. Of course, we are all familiar with the first book he wrote, namely scripture. But he has written a second book called creation." In his book, *The Incarnation of the Son of God*, Charles Gore, one of the most important theologians in the Anglican tradition, wrote,

> To believe in God is to move about the world… [recognizing that] God is in all things. There is no creature so small, but represents something of his goodness. [God] is disclosed in all graces and kinds of life: under the diverse modes of beauty, and truth, and goodness."

Indeed, God is powerfully revealed to us through creation. On July 15, 1978, two days after I turned 18, I stayed at a bed-and-breakfast in Oban, Scotland, run by a Mrs. Lewis. I headed overseas after high school with plans to train with a semi-professional soccer team in Aberdeen. My mother insisted, since I was postponing college and hoping to play soccer abroad, that I at least travel a bit as well. After locating the bed-and-breakfast, I walked down a stone staircase known to the locals as Jacob's Ladder to purchase some cheese, a loaf of bread and a carton of milk.

Sitting on the stone windowsill of my room, I listened to classical music on my transistor radio and watched as the sun slowly descended in the direction of the Islands of Mull and Iona, where Christianity came to Scotland in 563 CE. My parents were going through a difficult divorce. As I watched the brilliant sunset, it was if a veil had been lifted. I could literally see that something good would come forth from everything painful in my parents' marriage, in our family's life, in problems facing friends, and in even world events. I sensed that "all should be well," as Julian of Norwich famously wrote in her book, *Revelations of Divine Love*. That evening was a spiritual awakening, setting me on a course to become a committed Christian and eventually a priest. A few days later, I had a similar experience while watching the sheep graze by the waterside as the sun set in the Scottish Highlands.

Our encounters with God in creation remind us of the great connectedness of all living things and the harmonious design that God intends for us. Psalm 24 begins, "The earth is the Lord's and all that is in it." This understanding of the earth is echoed in Psalms 50:12, 89:11, and 98:8 and throughout scripture.

Millions of people know the power of discovering God not only in ancient churches, monasteries, and holy sites, but also in the surrounding landscapes. The high crosses of Ireland consecrate the surrounding hills and fields and remind visitors that they are standing on holy ground. All life is holy. The outdoors is indeed the handiwork of God. Who can venture through a forest of redwood trees or stand on a mountain overlooking the valleys below and not have a religious experience?

Climate change and global warming, however, are now affecting all of creation. They are the most pressing issues of our day. Other concerns are vital, but they will not matter if the planet becomes unsustainable for human life. Nature is resilient but delicate.

Today, humans are paying the price as we experience extreme weather and natural disasters: massive flooding, fires ravaging huge swaths of territory, rising sea levels, cyclones, tornadoes, and hurricanes devasting many regions, and massive water shortages. Water has become more precious than oil in many parts of the world, leading to massive displacements of people. Young people wonder what the future holds for them. We have obsessed with human freedom at the expense of the common good. Leaders in corporations, government, and those investing funds must take action to avoid reaching a point of no return.

In 1962, Rachel Carson published *Silent Spring*, which many claim set the foundation for the modern environmental movement. Carson's book analyzed the effects of many pesticides on the environment, DDT in particular. It also implicated the chemical industry and modern industrial society for the developing environmental crisis.

Four years later, historian Lynn White Jr. delivered an address to the American Association for the Advancement of Science in which he bluntly stated that Christianity "bears a huge burden of guilt for the devastation of nature in which the West has been engaged for centuries." His address generated a huge amount of debate.

White's premise was that the Judeo-Christian tradition "made it possible to exploit all nature in a mood of indifference to the feelings of natural objects." He cited the biblical command "to fill the earth and subdue it" (Genesis 1:28) as the ultimate proof that the Judeo-Christian tradition puts humans above the rest of creation and regards all other forms of life as subordinate. He maintained that this faulty understanding of scripture gave a green light for humans to dominate the earth.

White was a devout Christian. He did not intend his essay to be a general attack on the Judeo-Christian tradition but rather as a criticism to a particular strain of Christianity that he saw as supporting environmental degradation. Whereas animistic paganism viewed humans as part of nature, Christianity, said White, viewed humans as dominant over nature. This created a dualism that had not previously existed, desacralizing nature and paving the way for its destruction. Christianity, said White, made it possible to exploit nature with indifference to creation. He proposed Saint Francis as a model for how God intended humans to relate to nature. "I propose Francis as a patron saint of ecologists," he wrote.

In his article "Creation and Environment," Anglican theologian John Macquarrie challenged the blanket criticisms of the Judeo-Christian tradition as regards the environment. Macquarrie pointed to Genesis 9, where God makes a covenant with Noah after the flood. God speaks to Noah and says, "As for me, I am establishing my covenant with you and your descendants after you, and with every living creature that is with you, the birds, the domestic animals, and every animal of the earth with you, as many as came out of the ark" (Genesis 9:9-10).

He argued that this was a covenant to protect both humans and animals, not one to be viewed in terms of "domination" or "superiority" of humans over animals. Macquarrie maintained that Genesis 9 overrode the declarations found in Genesis 1 and 2. He also cited the celebration of nature found throughout the psalms and evidenced in other parts of the Bible that God's glory was manifested in all of creation.

French-American microbiologist, pathologist, and environmentalist René Dubos maintained Christians should look to Saint Benedict of Nursia, founder of the Benedictine monastic order, as a role model for interacting with creation. Dubos argued that Benedictines promoted manual labor and self-sufficient monasteries with a focus on the stewardship of all created things, including land and animals. He noted that when establishing monasteries, Benedictines drained swamps, created good farmland, and did not exploit the environment. Their work, said Dubos, was an act of "stewardship" and "a prayer which helps in recreating paradise out of chaotic wilderness." Benedict, said Dubos, represented the wise use of the land while Francis represented a utopian dream doomed to fail.

Since White's controversial article in 1966, environmental issues have become increasingly important with each passing year. Today, hardly a day passes where we do not read or hear about climate change and global warming. A recent United Nations report claims that the global average temperature will rise 2.7 degrees Celsius by century's end and notes that even if all countries meet their promised emissions cuts, this rise is likely to worsen extreme wildfires, droughts, and floods.

Despite the COVID-19 pandemic slowing the economy, shutting down businesses and drastically reducing air travel and other transportation, 2020 was the hottest year ever reported on the planet. The temperature in Death Valley reached 130 degrees. The most recorded wildfires in history burned over five million acres—a land mass equal to the entire area of Connecticut, Delaware, and Rhode Island combined.

David Pogue, who frequently hosts PBS's *Nova* science specials, discusses climate change and the greenhouse effect by showing a photograph of two dogs in a car. "If we want to reach people, we should call it the dog-in-the-car-effect. You come back to your car in the summer and it's boiling inside. Same exact thing: trapped infrared energy reflected from the sun. In the climate analogy, we are the dog," says Pogue. He shows a graph that starkly depicts the dramatic rise in levels of carbon dioxide.

Pogue sometimes exchanges the words "global warming" with "global weirding." "It's heat waves, freak snowstorms, flooding, water shortages, historic rains, droughts. We had the most hurricanes last season," he notes. "Nature is a network of interconnected systems. You can't turn one knob without affecting a bunch of other things."

In her article, "Christian Discipleship in the Environmental Crisis," Margot Hodson, one of our featured authors in this book, notes that there has been a 60% drop in vertebrate species since 1970. She writes, "Clearly something has gone badly wrong in our relationship with the Earth, and we have damaged and degraded the precious gift of creation that has been entrusted to us."

Indeed, "all of the world feels at risk, and most of it is," notes *The Economist*, adding that "even if everyone manages to honor today's firm pledges, large parts of the tropics risk becoming too hot for outdoor work. Coral reefs and livelihoods that depend on them will vanish, and the Amazon rainforest will become a ghost of itself. Severe harvest failures will be commonplace. Ice sheets in Antarctica and Greenland will shrink past the point of no return, promising sea rises measured not in millimeters, as today's are, but in meters." *The Economist* notes that progress toward reaching the goals of the Paris Agreement remain woefully inadequate.

In September of 2021, Pope Francis, Archbishop of Canterbury Justin Welby, and Ecumenical Patriarch Bartholomew issued a

The Creation Care Bible Challenge

joint statement for the first time, warning of the importance of environmental sustainability, its impact on poverty, and urgency for global cooperation. The statement read, "We call on everyone, whatever their belief or worldview, to endeavor to listen to the cry of the earth and of people who are poor, examining their behavior and pledging meaningful sacrifices for the sake of the earth which God has given to us." It concludes, "This is a critical moment. Our children's future and the future of our common home depend on it." They urge leaders to avoid focusing on short-term profits at the expense of long-term sustainability, adding, "God mandates: 'Choose life, so that you and your children might live'" (Deuteronomy 30:19)

Historian Lynn White was partially right to lay some of the blame for the environmental crisis at the feet of Christians, but we also can play a critical role in helping to reshape our self-understanding and attachment to the earth—while there is still time. Christianity demands that we critically rethink our lifestyles, our use of resources, our attachment to creation, and our theology and mission.

Margot Hodson notes, "The Protestant Reformation put emphasis on the first part of Romans 8; now we need a new 'Environmental Reformation' to place emphasis on the later part of Romans 8. Creation is groaning, and it has been stripped of its fullness by humanity. As Christians, we are called in Christ to act to enable fullness once more. To do this is to give glory to God." Like many things, we are finding that it has been in our scriptures all along. Only now are we discovering what God's Word has been saying to us all along.

The Rev. Marek P. Zabriskie
Founder of The Bible Challenge
Director of the Center for Biblical Studies
thecenterforbiblicalstudies.org

How to Read the Bible Prayerfully

Welcome to the Creation Care Bible Challenge. We are delighted that you are interested in reading God's life-transforming word. It will change and enrich your life. This book is an ideal resource for individuals, small groups, churches, and dioceses. Here are some suggestions to consider as you get started:

- You can begin the Creation Care Bible Challenge at any time of year. With 50 meditations, it's a perfect companion for each day of the season of Easter, but creation care itself is a year-long, day-in, day-out endeavor, and the book can be read at any period.

- Each day has a manageable amount of reading, a meditation, a few questions, and a prayer, written by one of many wonderful authors.

- We challenge you to read the Bible each day! This is a great spiritual discipline to establish.

- If you need more than fifty days to read through the Creation Care Bible Challenge, we support you in moving at the pace that works best for you. And if you want to keep going when you're done, a list of additional scripture citations is included in the back of the book. Keep reading!

- Many Bible Challenge participants read the Bible using their iPad, iPhone, Kindle, or Nook, or listen to the Bible on a mobile device using faithcomesthroughhearing.org, Audio.com, or Pandora radio. Find what works for you.

- Other resources for learning more about the Bible and engaging scripture can be found on our website,

ForwardMovement.org. In addition, you can find a list of resources at thecenterforbiblicalresources.org. The center also offers a Read the Bible in a Year program and reading plans for the New Testament, Psalms, and Proverbs.

- Because the Bible is not a newspaper, it is best to read it with a reverent spirit. We advocate a devotional approach to reading the Bible, rather than reading it as a purely intellectual or academic exercise.

- Before reading the Bible, take a moment of silence to put yourself in the presence of God. We then invite you to read this prayer written by Archbishop Thomas Cranmer:

Blessed Lord, who has caused all holy scriptures to be written for our learning: Grant us to hear them, read, mark, learn, and inwardly digest them, that we may embrace and ever hold fast the blessed hope of everlasting life, which you have given us in our Savior Jesus Christ; who lives and reigns with you and the Holy Spirit, one God, for ever and ever. Amen.

- Consider using the ancient monastic practice of *lectio divina*. In this form of Bible reading, you read the text and then meditate on a portion of it—be it a verse or two or even a single word. Mull over the words and their meaning. Then offer a prayer to God based on what you have read, how it has made you feel, or what it has caused you to ponder. Listen in silence for God to respond to your prayer.

- We encourage you to read in the morning, if possible, so that your prayerful reading may spiritually enliven the rest of your day. If you cannot read in the morning, read when you can later in the day. Try to carve out a regular time for your daily reading.

- One way to hold yourself accountable to reading God's Word is to form a group within your church or community— particularly any outreach and ministry groups. By participating in the Creation Care Bible Challenge together, you can support one another in your reading, discuss the Bible passages, ask questions, and share how God's word is transforming your life.

- Ask to have a notice printed in your church newsletter that you are starting a group to participate in the Creation Care Bible Challenge. Invite others to join you and gather regularly to discuss the readings, ask questions, and share how they transform your life. Visit the Center for Biblical Resources website to see more suggestions about how churches can participate in The Bible Challenge.

- Have fun and find spiritual peace and the joy that God desires for you in your daily reading. The Center for Biblical Studies aims to help you discover God's wisdom and to create a lifelong spiritual practice of daily Bible reading so that God may guide you through each day of your life.

- Once you've finished one complete reading of the Bible, start over and do it again. God may speak differently to you in each reading. Follow the example of U.S. President John Adams, who read through the Bible each year during his adult life. We highly advocate this practice.

- After participating in the Creation Care Bible Challenge, you will be more equipped to support and mentor others in reading the Bible—and to connect your ministry of advocacy and assistance with Holy Scripture.

We are thrilled that you are participating in The Bible Challenge. May God richly bless you as you prayerfully engage the scriptures each day. To learn more about The Bible Challenge, visit us at: thecenterforblicalstudies.org to see all of our resources.

The Creation Care Bible Challenge

A 50 Day Bible Challenge

Genesis 1:1-5

¹In the beginning when God created the heavens and the earth, ²the earth was a formless void and darkness covered the face of the deep, while a wind from God swept over the face of the waters.

³Then God said, "Let there be light"; and there was light. ⁴And God saw that the light was good; and God separated the light from the darkness. ⁵God called the light Day, and the darkness he called Night. And there was evening and there was morning, the first day.

Reflection

We are poignantly aware that God's narrative does not include us as the central cast of God's actions. We are a part of a greater work. We are created as part of God's cosmos, which begins before our arrival in the garden.

The central active word in this passage is "separated" or "divided." The better translation is "set apart for God's service." God's purpose of creation and creatures is to be *set apart to serve* as a reflection of God's self, beauty, and glory. The first to hear this text understood their contiguous role in the narrative and within the wider body of creation.

Today, we live within a different worldview. We see the spaces we occupy and the environment surrounding us as observable objects. We objectify others and God, so too we objectify the wider creation and its creatures. We naturally upend God's narrative. We interject humanity at the center of it, with God and creation existing for our benefit.

We hide from our sin—the polluting of God's intent. We pollute waterways and oceans, drive creatures to extinction, and make ourselves unwell. We create a 1.6 million square kilometer trash island in the Pacific (twice the size of Texas); we clutter Earth's orbit with 27,000 pieces of space debris and continue to launch future trash in the form of exploration tools onto other planets of God's making— with no plans for recapturing and recycling. Creation care is a cosmic issue and a reminder that science alone will not fix the problem before us.

God's beginning narrative reminds us that this planet and the cosmos are not ours and do not exist for our benefit but for God's. We are at once invited to realize our place within God's cosmic creation, and only then may we take part and tend and serve the Garden of God's making.

The Rt. Rev. C. Andrew "Andy" Doyle
Bishop of the Diocese of Texas
Houston, Texas

Questions

When you think of Genesis, what are the first pieces of the narrative that come to mind? How has that shaped your worldview of the whole text?

How might you do a fearless personal moral inventory that would open your eyes to our sin of pollution (personal and corporate)?

The Book of Common Prayer speaks of reconciliation as amending actions by means that bring comfort and counsel. What does repentance look like?

How might you participate within your family, your wider community, and the wider country to mend God's creation?

Prayer

God, who multiplied the blessing of creation through cosmic self-revelation, aid us in understanding our place within the body of creation. Give us courage to name our sin of pollution and strengthen us to set upon an individual and corporate pilgrimage to tend the cosmos as a blessing that reveals your beauty and glory to future generations. *Amen.*

Genesis 1:6-8

⁶And God said, "Let there be a dome in the midst of the waters, and let it separate the waters from the waters." ⁷So God made the dome and separated the waters that were under the dome from the waters that were above the dome. And it was so. ⁸God called the dome Sky. And there was evening and there was morning, the second day.

Reflection

I have always loved being in and with water—swimming, washing dishes, and taking long, hot showers. Maybe you have, too. Every human being comes from the watery world of the womb. Our bodies are mostly water. Water is as essential to our lives as the air we breathe. On day two in the book of Genesis, we read that out of a watery abyss, God places a dome in the midst of waters to separate the waters above from the waters below.

In the Godly Play method of presenting scripture stories, author Jerome Berryman clarifies just what water we are talking about in Genesis when he writes (and the storyteller says) in the creation story: "Now I don't mean just the water in a water glass or the water in a bathtub or shower. I don't even mean just the water in a river or a lake. I don't even mean just the water in the ocean or the water that comes down from the sky in rain. I mean all of the water that is water. This is the water that all the rest of the water comes from."

Then the storyteller shows the card with the firmament, dividing the waters. This powerful storytelling reminds me that water has never been added to the world since creation. It is the same water, now in vastly different places and arrangements than at creation.

During the pandemics of COVID-19, climate change, and racial injustice, I have been reminded that water justice is also essential to the flourishing of all creation. We have depended on water to wash our hands during the pandemic. Extreme flooding and hurricanes have increased this past year, as have extreme heat and fires, as climate change causes water shortage and damage. Communities of color are disproportionately affected by both climate change and unclean and unsafe drinking water.

The prophet Amos preached, "Let justice roll down like waters, and righteousness like an everflowing stream." How can I be more mindful of the gift of water on my island home? It is not a renewable resource. The amount has not changed since creation.

The Rev. Dr. Anita Louise Schell
Provisional Priest-in-Charge of St. Ann's Church
Old Lyme, Connecticut

Questions

Some have proposed adding a sixth response to the Baptismal Covenant in the Book of Common Prayer to address climate change and our duty to protect the beauty and integrity of all creation. Would such an addition to the baptismal liturgy change your understanding of baptism? If so, how?

In what watershed do you live? What significance does this watershed have for you and your neighborhood? What does justice rolling down like water and righteousness like an everflowing stream look like to you and your faith community?

Prayer

Almighty and ever generous God, you have given us the gift of water. We confess that we have not cared for this vital resource as a gift. Out of greed, we have polluted, squandered, consumed, and hoarded your precious gift. We pray that we may be restored to a right relationship with the waters above and the waters below. All this we pray in the name of the one who was called by you from the waters of his baptism, Jesus Christ, our Savior and Redeemer. *Amen.*

Genesis 1:24-28

24And God said, "Let the earth bring forth living creatures of every kind: cattle and creeping things and wild animals of the earth of every kind." And it was so. 25God made the wild animals of the earth of every kind, and the cattle of every kind, and everything that creeps upon the ground of every kind. And God saw that it was good.

26Then God said, "Let us make humankind in our image, according to our likeness; and let them have dominion over the fish of the sea, and over the birds of the air, and over the cattle, and over all the wild animals of the earth, and over every creeping thing that creeps upon the earth."

27So God created humankind in his image, in the image of God he created them; male and female he created them. 28God blessed them, and God said to them, "Be fruitful and multiply, and fill the earth and subdue it; and have dominion over the fish of the sea and over the birds of the air and over every living thing that moves upon the earth."

Reflection

It is often missed (and we may wonder why) that the sixth day of creation begins with God making all the animals—wild animals and domestic animals, but this day doesn't end there. God declares that these animals are good, but the sixth day of creation doesn't close until after God makes humans. We share the sixth day with the wild animals and cattle!

Granted, God lavishes more directions on us, and those directions, as many have interpreted them, have brought sharp criticisms from environmentalists. The words that are most problematic are "subdue" and "dominion." A famous essay, "The Historical Roots of Our Ecological Crisis," written by Lynn White in 1966, laid the blame for the rampant destruction of the environment squarely on the shoulders of Christians who have interpreted this passage as license to be Earth conquistadores.

In the years since 1966, many interpreters have provided a truer meaning of the charge given to us. Let me point out that when we combine the sharing of a day of creation with animals, with the fact that "dominion" and "domicile" come from the same ancient root, a word meaning house, we come up with a home that is made of time and space. And when we look back further in Genesis 1, we see that God created the heavens as a dome, a great house.

Our task, then, is to be a householder, with all the animals as part of the household with us. Think of dorm parents. We need to provide for and care for and indeed get along with our housemates. If we fail, our contract may not be renewed.

The Rt. Rev. Marc Andrus
Bishop of the Diocese of California
San Francisco, California

Questions

What, in the way humans are created, suits us to be heads of the household we share with other animals?

How does thinking of the animals of the earth, including domestic animals, as members of the same household with us change your views of life?

Can you think of one way you can change your thinking and doing after looking at this passage from Genesis?

Prayer

Dear God, we pray that your love will become the energy molding our treatment of the other creatures with whom we share Earth, our island home. Help us to be humane, patient, and kind to all. When we fail, lead us to amendment of life. Bless all life in the name of Jesus Christ our Savior. *Amen.*

Genesis 2:4b-8

[4]These are the generations of the heavens and the earth when they were created. In the day that the LORD God made the earth and the heavens, [5]when no plant of the field was yet in the earth and no herb of the field had yet sprung up—for the LORD God had not caused it to rain upon the earth, and there was no one to till the ground; [6]but a stream would rise from the earth, and water the whole face of the ground—[7]then the LORD God formed man from the dust of the ground, and breathed into his nostrils the breath of life; and the man became a living being.

[8]And the LORD God planted a garden in Eden, in the east; and there he put the man whom he had formed.

Reflection

The story begins with a garden. God takes the *adama*, the Hebrew word for dirt or soil or earth, and forms it into *adam,* a creature made of the earth. And God breathes into this creature, and it becomes a living being. The word for God, YHWH, literally means "I Am," but it is also your breath. For the ancients, life began when a baby sucked air into its lungs, and it ended when an old person slowly ceased breathing. The word for breath was life and soul, and it was also God. It was God living in us, breathing into us.

To be well, we need to begin with one simple thing: our breath. Begin by just breathing. Remember the gift that it is to breathe. A man in my congregation just finished a battle with testicular cancer and is in remission. Ironically, this battle made him grateful and well. He gives thanks for every breath.

The second thing that we need for wellness is the earth. We are part of the earth. We were meant to be outside and to live with this beautiful creation that God has made. Wellness must begin with a return to the breath and to the ground. To plant, to sit under a tree, to breathe. Stick your hands in the dirt. Go for a walk. Breathe under a tree. It all began with us on the ground, in the ground.

God also clearly says that it is not good for this *adam* to be alone. So, God makes animals. In Hebrew, the word for animal is sustainer. In this story, animals were originally created as company to sustain us and help us.

And God gives the *adam* dominion over the animals, not to lord it over them and not to eat them but to watch over them, protect them, and care for them as a parent would care for a child. One step to wellness may often be to introduce an animal into a person's life and let that person care for and love that animal. It is a fundamental part of the recipe of what it once looked like for us in Eden.

Notice too that every physical need of the human is taken care of: food, comfort, beauty. This tells us that it is essential that our basic physical needs are met in order to be well. We cannot find wellness if we are deprived of food, or sleep, or safety. These are essentials and must be addressed before everything else.

How do we begin to return to wellness? Begin with your breath, then walk outside and touch the ground, and then, maybe, consider caring for an animal. It is a simple recipe, made in the Garden of Eden itself, a recipe for health and wholeness. And God provides all the ingredients.

The Very Rev. Kate Moorehead
Dean of St. John's Cathedral
Jacksonville, Florida

Questions

Try sitting still and listening to your breath. Do you hear how it sounds like Yahweh? What does it mean to you that the name for God is your very breath?

Try taking a walk outside. Do you find yourself marveling at the beauty of God's creation? Why do you sometimes walk outside and forget to notice?

Do you have an animal, a pet? If so, how does that pet sustain you?

Have you ever thought that the relationship between a person and animals predates the relationship between human beings?

Prayer

Eternal God, Maker of the heavens and the earth, Creator and Sustainer of all life, help us to return to the way in which you made us, to appreciate the simple act of breathing, to walk in nature and touch the earth itself, to hold a pet or marvel at a tree. Forgive us from the distractions of this life that tempt us to forget who we are, the busyness that makes us sick and isolated from you and one another. Help us return to the simple state of Eden, where we live in gratitude for this beautiful earth that you have given us, and from this place of gratitude, may we learn to revere and care for this earth and all that is in it. In Christ's name we pray. *Amen.*

Genesis 2:15-22

[15]The LORD God took the man and put him in the garden of Eden to till it and keep it.

[16]And the LORD God commanded the man, "You may freely eat of every tree of the garden; [17]but of the tree of the knowledge of good and evil you shall not eat, for in the day that you eat of it you shall die."

[18]Then the LORD God said, "It is not good that the man should be alone; I will make him a helper as his partner." [19]So out of the ground the LORD God formed every animal of the field and every bird of the air, and brought them to the man to see what he would call them; and whatever the man called every living creature, that was its name. [20]The man gave names to all cattle, and to the birds of the air, and to every animal of the field; but for the man there was not found a helper as his partner.

[21]So the LORD God caused a deep sleep to fall upon the man, and he slept; then he took one of his ribs and closed up its place with flesh.

[22]And the rib that the LORD God had taken from the man he made into a woman and brought her to the man.

Reflection

Once upon a time, we might have interpreted the story of Adam naming the animals as another biblical justification for human alienation from nature: God presents animals to the man, and the man supplies their names, thereby asserting domination and control over them. We might have concluded that this text provides a divine mandate for human beings to exploit and plunder the natural world.

But we cannot settle for interpretations like that. When ecosystems are near collapse, species are going extinct, and populations of animals are vanishing in what scientists term a "biological annihilation," this story must be read afresh. It tells us that humanity is built for loving relationship. God knows that "it is not good that the man should be alone." We cannot exist by ourselves or for ourselves. God created us to flourish within a connected, living world.

God forms "every animal of the field and every bird of the air" out of the same dust from which Adam was formed. Humans and our nonhuman relations are intrinsically linked: we spring from the same soil; we're made from the same stuff. God brings the animals to the man "to see what he would call them." Naming a living creature, or discovering the name that it's already been given, requires care and curiosity.

I imagine Adam contemplating each God-given creature one by one and taking time to get to know and interact with it before deciding on its name. How can you discover the name of one plant or another or distinguish one bird from another until you've looked at it closely? I like to think that he knew how to look—that his naming of the animals was a sign of his willingness to abide with them and learn from them. The best words for anything come only after we have experienced it deeply, not before.

When Adam finally finds his partner, bone of his bones and flesh of his flesh, their shared task as human beings is to "to till and keep" the earth—to mediate divine blessings to other creatures.

The Rev. Dr. Margaret Bullitt-Jonas
Missioner for Creation Care for the
Episcopal Diocese of Western Massachusetts and
Southern New England Conference, United Church of Christ
Creation Care Advisor for the Episcopal Diocese of Massachusetts
Northampton, Massachusetts

Questions

Would learning to identify ten kinds of local trees, plants, and birds help you form a closer relationship with God's creation? Would learning the names of creatures now on the brink of extinction affect your motivation to bless and protect them?

If you have a yard, can you turn it into a conservation corridor?

How is God inviting you to live in a more conscious, just, and gentle relationship with the rest of the natural world?

Prayer

Gracious and loving God, you formed all creatures from out of the ground: help us recognize our deep kinship with other living beings and greet them with the same care and curiosity we would feel in meeting them for the first time. Give us the courage to amend our lives so that the web of life as it has evolved will not vanish from the earth. In Christ's name and presence, we pray. *Amen*.

The Creation Care Bible Challenge

Genesis 9:8-17

⁸Then God said to Noah and to his sons with him, ⁹"As for me, I am establishing my covenant with you and your descendants after you, ¹⁰and with every living creature that is with you, the birds, the domestic animals, and every animal of the earth with you, as many as came out of the ark. ¹¹I establish my covenant with you, that never again shall all flesh be cut off by the waters of a flood, and never again shall there be a flood to destroy the earth."

¹²God said, "This is the sign of the covenant that I make between me and you and every living creature that is with you, for all future generations: ¹³I have set my bow in the clouds, and it shall be a sign of the covenant between me and the earth. ¹⁴When I bring clouds over the earth and the bow is seen in the clouds, ¹⁵I will remember my covenant that is between me and you and every living creature of all flesh; and the waters shall never again become a flood to destroy all flesh. ¹⁶When the bow is in the clouds, I will see it and remember the everlasting covenant between God and every living creature of all flesh that is on the earth." ¹⁷God said to Noah, "This is the sign of the covenant that I have established between me and all flesh that is on the earth."

Reflection

Noah's ark is far more than a children's story. It tells us vital biblical truths about God's priorities at a time of human sin and ecological devastation. Simply to ask the question, "Who gets saved?" leads to an understanding that God's purposes are far wider than ours and the churches tend to be—and include concern for every living creature.

The climax of the Noah account is God's covenant in Genesis 9:8-17. This is the first explicit biblical covenant, and it sets the context for the later covenants with Abraham and Moses. In this covenant, made through the sign of a rainbow, God resets how things are to be in a world that is no longer Eden. Human sin has upset the order of things, and although the flood has washed away much of the evil on the earth, relationships remain damaged, with fear and accountability characterizing human-animal relations.

It is, therefore, remarkable just who God's covenant is with. The partners in God's unilateral declaration of care and blessing include not only humans but also, repeatedly, the whole of life on earth. Seven times in the Hebrew text, God affirms that his saving covenant includes "every living creature" (Genesis 9, verses 10, 12, 15, 16), "all life" (11, 17), and even "the earth" (13).

Here we have a God who is passionate about biodiversity! In the light of this passage, we need to rethink the extent of the gospel and our mission as Christians. God's Good News includes not only people but also all creatures, and we, like Noah, are called to work for the flourishing of all life on earth. Unless we all flourish, no one and no thing can flourish.

The Rev. Dr. Dave Bookless
Director of Theology at A Rocha International
Priest-in-Charge of St. Mary's Norwood Green
London, England

Questions

Why have we consistently overlooked the significance of nonhuman animals in God's saving plans and in God's covenant? What challenge does this bring to our priorities as Christians and as churches?

What about our lifestyles? How can we live in a way that recognizes God's covenant relationship with all creatures and encourages the flourishing of all life on earth?

Prayer

God of creation and covenant, we praise you for your servant Noah, whom you called to serve you in rescuing life on earth. Teach us to share your heart of compassion for every living creature. Enable us to change our priorities and lifestyles to align with your love for all that you have made, through Jesus Christ our Lord. *Amen.*

Genesis 28:10-17

[10]Jacob left Beer-sheba and went toward Haran. [11]He came to a certain place and stayed there for the night, because the sun had set. Taking one of the stones of the place, he put it under his head and lay down in that place. [12]And he dreamed that there was a ladder set up on the earth, the top of it reaching to heaven; and the angels of God were ascending and descending on it. [13]And the LORD stood beside him and said, "I am the LORD, the God of Abraham your father and the God of Isaac; the land on which you lie I will give to you and to your offspring; [14]and your offspring shall be like the dust of the earth, and you shall spread abroad to the west and to the east and to the north and to the south; and all the families of the earth shall be blessed in you and in your offspring. [15]Know that I am with you and will keep you wherever you go, and will bring you back to this land; for I will not leave you until I have done what I have promised you."

[16]Then Jacob woke from his sleep and said, "Surely the LORD is in this place—and I did not know it!" [17]And he was afraid, and said, "How awesome is this place! This is none other than the house of God, and this is the gate of heaven."

Reflection

When Jacob dreams of angels ascending and descending a staircase to heaven, he is far from his homeland, his mother, and his religious community and their sacred shrines. But as he wakes up, Jacob declares, "Surely the Lord is in this place—and I did not know it!" He realizes God is not confined to communities and shrines but is present even in this wild land, though this reality is already well-established in the Hebrew narrative.

The Old Testament emphasizes the state of the land itself as an index of the people's faithfulness to God. Old Testament scholar Ellen Davis writes about this in her brilliant book, *Scripture, Culture, and Agriculture: An Agrarian Reading of Scripture*. She says that when the Israelites wander far from God, the land suffers. "Thorns and briars abound (Genesis 3:17-19); rain is withheld (Deuteronomy 11:11-17; 28:24); the land languishes and mourns (Isaiah 16:8; 33:9; Hosea 4:3)."

By contrast, when harmony with God is restored, the land overflows with good things and is "lush with growth," say the psalms and the prophets. There is a direct correlation between how the people relate to the creation and all its bounty and how they relate to their creator. Today's extreme weather patterns, fires, floods, and droughts serve as glaring warning signals that we have drifted far from harmony in our relationship with the earth and its Creator.

With the exception of most of humanity, nature abides by basic laws and strategies for survival that, if humankind were to return to them as guiding principles in our endeavors, might solve nearly every environmental challenge we are up against today. Nature uses only the energy it needs, and most of its energy comes from sunlight.

Nature never wastes anything but recycles everything. Nature adapts to its local place and does not destroy its essential resources. Nature rewards cooperation within and between species. In every ecosystem, diversity is the key to all life forms flourishing. This wisdom of nature mirrors the wisdom of the God who creates it all.

The Rev. Elizabeth Garnsey
Associate Rector at St. Mark's Episcopal Church
New Canaan, Connecticut

Questions _____

Go outdoors and observe the above survival strategies at work among plants, animals, and insects. How is God calling you to mirror these ways of being in your own life?

In what ways can we see the wisdom of God in our recycling bins and trash cans, in the food we eat, in the energy we use to heat and cool our homes, in how we travel, in what we choose to buy and throw away, in how we share resources with others?

Prayer _____

Dear God, awaken us to see your wisdom at work in the world you have made. Teach us to see our important but relatively small place in the grand created order. Help us to learn the wisdom of our fellow creatures so that, like them, we may thrive and flourish by living within the means of the earth's abundant resources, to your honor and glory. *Amen.*

Exodus 3:1-12

¹Moses was keeping the flock of his father-in-law Jethro, the priest of Midian; he led his flock beyond the wilderness, and came to Horeb, the mountain of God. ²There the angel of the LORD appeared to him in a flame of fire out of a bush; he looked, and the bush was blazing, yet it was not consumed. ³Then Moses said, "I must turn aside and look at this great sight, and see why the bush is not burned up." ⁴When the LORD saw that he had turned aside to see, God called to him out of the bush, "Moses, Moses!" And he said, "Here I am." ⁵Then he said, "Come no closer! Remove the sandals from your feet, for the place on which you are standing is holy ground." ⁶He said further, "I am the God of your father, the God of Abraham, the God of Isaac, and the God of Jacob." And Moses hid his face, for he was afraid to look at God.

⁷Then the LORD said, "I have observed the misery of my people who are in Egypt; I have heard their cry on account of their taskmasters. Indeed, I know their sufferings, ⁸and I have come down to deliver them from the Egyptians, and to bring them up out of that land to a good and broad land, a land flowing with milk and honey, to the country of the Canaanites, the Hittites, the Amorites, the Perizzites, the Hivites, and the Jebusites. ⁹The cry of the Israelites has now come to me; I have also seen how the Egyptians oppress them. ¹⁰So come, I will send you to Pharaoh to bring my people, the Israelites, out of Egypt."

[11]But Moses said to God, "Who am I that I should go to Pharaoh, and bring the Israelites out of Egypt?" [12]He said, "I will be with you; and this shall be the sign for you that it is I who sent you: when you have brought the people out of Egypt, you shall worship God on this mountain."

Reflection

During COVID-19, we were not able to worship God in our churches, and many people spent more time in nature. It was a safe place to meet up with friends and to find peace when we were stressed. Some began to experience the presence of God in a new and deeper way.

In this passage, Moses is faced with an overwhelming challenge—to rescue his people from Egypt. He feels totally underskilled for the task ahead. And yet, by meeting with God on the mountain, his fears are put to rest, and he is empowered to go back down the mountain and take up the challenge. During his time on the holy ground of the mountain, he encounters God and is strengthened spiritually and mentally to take the lead in bringing God's people to freedom.

Jesus also goes to the mountain to pray after times of stress. Jesus spends a lot of time in synagogues, teaching, healing, and debating the interpretation of the Torah. However, we also see that spending time with God in nature is also very important to him. Jesus starts his ministry with a forty-day retreat in the wilderness, and he often chooses to go and pray in nature at particularly difficult times. For instance, after receiving the news of the brutal murder of his close friend, John the Baptist, followed by a marathon ministry day of preaching and feeding an enormous crowd of people, Jesus goes up onto a mountain to pray alone (Matthew 14:23). After he fights with the Pharisees and teachers of the law, Jesus goes out to the mountain and spends the night in prayer to God (Luke 6:12).

Like Moses and Jesus, may we experience the presence of God in nature so that we can come back down the mountain and take up the challenges that lie ahead of us.

The Rev. Dr. Rachel Mash
Environmental Coordinator of the Anglican Church of Southern Africa
Secretary of the Anglican Communion Environmental Network
Cape Town, South Africa

Questions

Where in nature have you felt closest to God? Why is that place important to you?

What changes can you make in your life balance so that you can experience more of the presence of God through creation?

Prayer

Creator God, when we are overwhelmed, may we feel your presence, for we are standing on holy ground. When we are afraid, may we hear your voice in the sound of the roaring breakers. When our hearts are broken, may we feel your touch in the sun on our face and the wind on our skin. When we are weary, let us lie down by the living waters and be refreshed. *Amen*.

Exodus 23:10-12

[10]For six years you shall sow your land and gather in its yield; [11]but the seventh year you shall let it rest and lie fallow, so that the poor of your people may eat; and what they leave the wild animals may eat. You shall do the same with your vineyard, and with your olive orchard. [12]Six days you shall do your work, but on the seventh day you shall rest, so that your ox and your donkey may have relief, and your homeborn slave and the resident alien may be refreshed.

Reflection

Like much of the Bible, these verses run counter to our modern proclivities. Leaving a piece of land to lie fallow sounds wasteful, foolish even. Surely, with our advanced technologies, tools, and chemicals, we can force the soil to nurture and produce bigger and better crops. We can find ways to squeeze out every last nutrient; we pride ourselves on such efficiency.

But these verses remind us of the importance of sabbath. In Genesis, we read that God rested on the seventh day, and here in Exodus, we receive instruction to not only let the fields lie fallow in the seventh year but also that we too should rest on the seventh day.

From an agricultural perspective, this sabbath practice makes scientific sense. A fallowing period gives the soil a chance to regenerate and the nutrients that have been leached by crops to replenish. While nothing appears to be happening during this time, underneath the soil is a symphony of re-creation. Worms burrow through the dirt, creating paths for water and air and depositing nutrient-rich excrement. Potassium and phosphorus, critical elements for growth, rise back to the surface, and levels of carbon, nitrogen, and other organic matter increase. In the subsequent years, these fields produce higher-yields, studies have shown.

This shouldn't be surprising. We see in our own lives that our tired, worn-out selves can't produce the same results as when we are rested and refreshed. As we embrace the care of creation as part of our spiritual calling, we must find ways to re-prioritize rest and refreshment, in the earth and in our lives.

Richelle Thompson
Managing Editor, Forward Movement
Fort Thomas, Kentucky

Questions

If you have a garden, have you considered letting part of it lie fallow? How can you incorporate this practice in your personal life? In your church or community?

How does the concept of sabbath fit within creation care? What else could benefit from the same model of periods of lying fallow?

How do you personally respond to this directive to rest and refresh?

Prayer

Gracious God, you give us the tools and instruction we need to grow and flourish. Create in us a right spirit that we may embrace these seasons of work and rest, in the earth and in our lives. May we ever abide by your commands and seek your wisdom. In your name we pray. *Amen.*

Leviticus 19:9-10

⁹When you reap the harvest of your land, you shall not reap to the very edges of your field, or gather the gleanings of your harvest. ¹⁰You shall not strip your vineyard bare or gather the fallen grapes of your vineyard; you shall leave them for the poor and the alien: I am the LORD your God.

Reflection

In an effort to counter the triple global effects of COVID-19, climate change, and conflicts, families, communities, workplaces, and countries may be tempted to exploit God's creation beyond its rhythms of sustainability and to forget their moral responsibility for the most vulnerable in society.

However, God's ethical code commands landowners to be good stewards of God's resources and relationships by not exploiting the land beyond its limits and allowing the poor and the foreign to glean from their farms.

In sparing the land, they fulfill God's holiness as their creator, and in leaving room for the poor and foreign residents to work, they provide people with dignified livelihoods. In challenging times, living simply so that many can simply live is an act of faith and good stewardship.

Listening to God who speaks through creation and learning the language of nature can help heal the planet. Likewise, limiting our income so that increased means of production are generated for many, especially for the youth, can strengthen homegrown solutions for social unrest and forced migrations.

Jesus has equated the love of God (Deuteronomy 6:4-5) with love to the neighbor (Leviticus 19:18) and made it the foundation of all moral requirements (Mark 12:30-31).

In response to Jesus's call to love our neighbor, we have seen a worldwide movement of solidarity and generosity. However, in fully envisioning restoration in a post-COVID world, we will need to move beyond charity to full inclusion and participation in God's family.

The Rt. Rev. Manuel Ernesto
Bishop of the Anglican Diocese of Nampula
Marrere, Mozambique

Questions

Conflicts, climate change, and more recently COVID-19 have resulted in the loss of livelihoods and forced many young people to migrate. If you are a refugee living in a foreign country, community, or neighborhood, what practical schemes exist to help young people to move beyond charity and begin to support themselves?

If you live in your own country, community, or neighborhood, what practical means exist to prevent young people from becoming endangered?

What can countries, communities, or neighborhoods do to foster more inclusion and active participation across social and national boundaries?

Prayer

Generous and loving God, freely you gifted us with abundant resources from your creation and joyful relationships with your son Jesus. Make us good stewards of your creation and let us be mindful of the needs and dignity of the most vulnerable in our communities. *Amen.*

Leviticus 25:1-7

¹The LORD spoke to Moses on Mount Sinai, saying: ²Speak to the people of Israel and say to them: When you enter the land that I am giving you, the land shall observe a sabbath for the LORD. ³Six years you shall sow your field, and six years you shall prune your vineyard, and gather in their yield; ⁴but in the seventh year there shall be a sabbath of complete rest for the land, a sabbath for the LORD: you shall not sow your field or prune your vineyard. ⁵You shall not reap the aftergrowth of your harvest or gather the grapes of your unpruned vine: it shall be a year of complete rest for the land. ⁶You may eat what the land yields during its sabbath—you, your male and female slaves, your hired and your bound laborers who live with you; ⁷for your livestock also, and for the wild animals in your land all its yield shall be for food.

Reflection

The book of Leviticus can be thought of as God's how-to manual. In this passage from Leviticus, God is instructing Moses—and through him, the Israelites, along with the rest of us—on how to keep our covenant with him. Central to God's message is the concept of sabbath.

Many of us think of the sabbath in personal terms. Are we taking a break? Are we exercising self-care? All that is important, of course. God really does want us to take care of ourselves—we are, after all, his creation. However, of equal or more importance is how we take care of the rest of God's creation. This is what God is concerned about within this passage.

We are stewards of that creation. Are we giving it a sabbath? Are we refraining from draining every last drop of nutrients from the soil? The evidence would suggest we are not. Too often, we turn our considerable God-given gifts and energy to exploiting what God has entrusted to us so that we can lead more convenient and abundant lives, whether that is higher crop yields using damaging chemicals or letting our faucet drip because we can't get around to fixing it.

In Leviticus, God is asking us to do something more difficult. He is asking us to defer the gratification of our needs for the greater good of creation, which includes all of us made in his image.

One is reminded of the famous marshmallow experiment. In this experiment, a child is placed in a room and offered a treat. However, the child is told that if they wait for a fixed period of time and don't eat the treat sitting in front of them, they will receive two treats of their choice. The experiment showed that children who were able to defer gratification, even just for fifteen minutes, had better life outcomes.

In Leviticus, God is saying much the same thing to us. Namely, if we are willing to give creation a sabbath and defer our gratification, even for just one year out of seven, it will be better for everyone. Good environmental stewardship isn't just good for creation; it's good for us.

Rob Radtke
President & CEO of Episcopal Relief & Development
New York City, New York

Questions _____

Where do you see the exploitation of creation in your daily life?

In what ways can you provide a sabbath for creation?

How does giving creation a sabbath bring benefits to you and your loved ones?

Prayer _____

God, you invite us to be your partners in the stewardship of your creation. Give us the will to hear your voice as you ask us to defer our immediate desires and curb our appetites for the benefit of creation and humanity as a whole. Help us provide creation with a sabbath from meeting our demands so that we, as your stewards, may ensure your creation's abundance for future generations. *Amen.*

Leviticus 25:8-12

⁸You shall count off seven weeks of years, seven times seven years, so that the period of seven weeks of years gives forty-nine years. ⁹Then you shall have the trumpet sounded loud; on the tenth day of the seventh month—on the day of atonement—you shall have the trumpet sounded throughout all your land. ¹⁰And you shall hallow the fiftieth year and you shall proclaim liberty throughout the land to all its inhabitants. It shall be a jubilee for you: you shall return, every one of you, to your property and every one of you to your family. ¹¹That fiftieth year shall be a jubilee for you: you shall not sow, or reap the aftergrowth, or harvest the unpruned vines. ¹²For it is a jubilee; it shall be holy to you: you shall eat only what the field itself produces.

Reflection

Many years ago, at a dinner celebrating the 250th birthday of St. Louis, I was seated next to a tribal elder from the Wa Zha Zhe (Osage) nation. At one point, driven by feelings of shame and desire to ease my own discomfort, I commented that it must be difficult to be at what was essentially a celebration of "when we took your land."

I had hoped for words of absolution, recognition that I was one of the good, enlightened white people. Instead, after listening patiently, my dinner companion paused, sighed, and then said with gentleness and love: "This is where you always get it wrong. You didn't take our land. It wasn't ours then. It isn't yours now. The land is always the land."

This passage is an accommodation. The law that Moses handed down presumes the concept of property, of ownership. It also knows that where there is ownership, there will be inequity: someone will always own more, and someone will always own less. There needs to be an accommodation: every fiftieth year, those who have become indebted and enslaved because of inequity are to be set free.

During this year of Jubilee, the land does not belong to anyone. It is not to be harvested. The produce, whatever it naturally yields, belongs to everyone.

The land is the land.

The earliest followers of the revolutionary and resurrected Jesus understood this concept.

"All who believed were together and had all things in common; they would sell their possessions and goods and distribute the proceeds to all, as any had need." (Acts 2:44-45).

What is revolutionary about Jesus, and what we as the church are most afraid to preach, is the truth that tribal elder imparted to me that evening.

"Go, sell what you own, and give the money to the poor, and you will have treasure in heaven; then come, follow me" (Mark 10:21).

There is no ownership. Ownership only leads to pain and inequity.

The land is not theirs. The land is not ours. The land is always the land.

The Rev. Mike Kinman
Rector of All Saints Church
Pasadena, California

Questions

What feels fearful and what feels liberating about having no property and no concept of ownership?

What would our faith communities look like if we lived Jubilee every year?

What fear is stopping us? What love can set us free?

Prayer

Great Breath of God, you create all that has been, all that is, and all that will be. Tune our bodies, minds, and spirits to the music of the land. Free us from seeing creation as property to be owned instead of abundance to be shared and celebrated. May the spirit of Jubilee inhabit us that all may thrive in the reality of enough. *Amen.*

Deuteronomy 8:1-10

¹This entire commandment that I command you today you must diligently observe, so that you may live and increase, and go in and occupy the land that the LORD promised on oath to your ancestors. ²Remember the long way that the LORD your God has led you these forty years in the wilderness, in order to humble you, testing you to know what was in your heart, whether or not you would keep his commandments. ³He humbled you by letting you hunger, then by feeding you with manna, with which neither you nor your ancestors were acquainted, in order to make you understand that one does not live by bread alone, but by every word that comes from the mouth of the LORD. ⁴The clothes on your back did not wear out and your feet did not swell these forty years. ⁵Know then in your heart that as a parent disciplines a child so the LORD your God disciplines you. ⁶Therefore keep the commandments of the LORD your God, by walking in his ways and by fearing him. ⁷For the LORD your God is bringing you into a good land, a land with flowing streams, with springs and underground waters welling up in valleys and hills, ⁸a land of wheat and barley, of vines and fig trees and pomegranates, a land of olive trees and honey, ⁹a land where you may eat bread without scarcity, where you will lack nothing, a land whose stones are iron and from whose hills you may mine copper.

¹⁰You shall eat your fill and bless the LORD your God for the good land that he has given you.

Reflection

To meditate on the promise of a good land promised by God in this passage is to face the reality of the devastation we humans have brought to the earth. To consider the bounty we freely received and mistook for our due is the beginning of lamentation.

Let us pause to list in our minds three or four things we use freely. Let us practice gratitude for these things and, out of that gratitude, determine how we might be better stewards in our families, communities, countries, and our global community.

We are connected to one another, as the earth's systems are interrelated. This is the Gaia Hypothesis, which holds the earth is a single living system and altering one piece of it sends ripples through the whole.

Eliza Griswold
Pulitzer Prize Winning Author, Poet, and Journalist
Philadelphia, Pennsylvania

Questions

What have I taken as my due from the earth?

Where can I practice gratitude for the earth and what does that look like?

What does my family's carbon footprint look like?

Prayer

Dear Earth, forgive us our trespasses, that we may acknowledge the harms we have done and free ourselves to listen to your lamentations in the air, soil, and storms, and find solutions to your healing and our own. *Amen.*

Job 12:1-10

¹Then Job answered: ²"No doubt you are the people, and wisdom will die with you. ³But I have understanding as well as you; I am not inferior to you. Who does not know such things as these? ⁴I am a laughingstock to my friends; I, who called upon God and he answered me, a just and blameless man, I am a laughingstock. ⁵Those at ease have contempt for misfortune, but it is ready for those whose feet are unstable.

⁶The tents of robbers are at peace, and those who provoke God are secure, who bring their God in their hands. ⁷But ask the animals, and they will teach you; the birds of the air, and they will tell you; ⁸ask the plants of the earth, and they will teach you; and the fish of the sea will declare to you. ⁹Who among all these does not know that the hand of the LORD has done this? ¹⁰In his hand is the life of every living thing and the breath of every human being."

Reflection

The laughter is deafening when inquiries about your responsibility of care for ME (Mother Earth) are made. I feel distant from you when you sparingly mention ME as a part of your past, present, and future when I have been yours since time began. We are growing apart. Your compassion for ME during my increased illness is somewhat absent, which upsets my whole family. Just ask them. They will tell you!

You never ask ME if I am satisfied in this relationship, and you have never told ME that I matter. Some say that it is only ME that is struggling with this, and rumor has it that you have fallen for something that satisfies you more. Then Eliphaz the Temanite, Bildad the Shuhite, and Zophar the Naamathite laugh at me. Despite my equal aptitude and astute understanding of things, there is contempt toward ME because God approves. Even those who respect ME more are subject to your ignorance!

We have discerned that your appetite for the "highs" in life is satisfied by another. This quest for something that flows not from my fountain of love leaves ME filled with grief and pain. How can I possibly compete? Although I give to you all that is given to ME by God, your heart has never been mine alone.

It would be a comfort, though, if you turned to the Lord and asked what was intended for ME in this relationship. The chasm in our shared designation widens daily. The encroaching estrangement leaves ME gasping for the breath that we were all to share. Submitting my whole being to the Lord, in search of what it will take for ME to go on, has rendered us with the conclusion that you love ME no more.

My family prays in the hope that you seek God's counsel in how to reconcile, restore, and renew your relationship with ME. Teachings, declarations, and stories of ME are free to upload, and if your connection is too weak, please feel free to contact ME at anytime, anywhere.

The Rev. Jacynthia Murphy
Operations Support Manager, General Synod Office of the Anglican Church in Aotearoa, New Zealand, and Polynesia
and the Māori Council of Churches
Auckland, New Zealand

Questions

They had no right to presume that he was of less stature with God than they were, and Job chooses to use cutting sarcasm and puzzling enigmas to get his point across. How is this a workable strategy for us today?

It sometimes appears that those who are not honorable prosper more, and Job attributes their prosperity to the hand of God. So, why not believe that God also allows the righteous to suffer?

Job knew that God had given permission for terrible things to happen to him. He accepted and declared that "nature" would have all the answers. How so?

Prayer

Kaitiaki, carer of all things, we praise you for all that we coexist with, respectfully utilize, and enthusiastically enjoy. We give eternal thanks for the created order you have generously bequeathed us. Grant us the foresight and wisdom to appreciate it, learn from it, and leave it as pristine as when we received it. Eternally yours in the image you have created us, we honor you. *Amen.*

Job 14:7-12

⁷For there is hope for a tree, if it is cut down, that it will sprout again, and that its shoots will not cease. ⁸Though its root grows old in the earth, and its stump dies in the ground, ⁹yet at the scent of water it will bud and put forth branches like a young plant. ¹⁰But mortals die, and are laid low; humans expire, and where are they? ¹¹As waters fail from a lake, and a river wastes away and dries up, ¹²so mortals lie down and do not rise again; until the heavens are no more, they will not awake or be roused out of their sleep.

Reflection

Job's friends had told him that he suffered because of his sins. He responds by arguing to them—and to God—that he is an innocent sufferer. His defense in the first verses of chapter 14 appeals to facts of the human condition, that mortals are short-lived and full of troubles, like flowers that blossom and wither away. The floral appeal inspires further natural imagery. At least, Job says, there is hope for a tree. Even if cut down, it may send out new shoots, and the scent of water may revive it. Human beings, in contrast, die and are no more. Christian readers may lament the absence of resurrection hope and regard Job as rather optimistic about the fate of trees. Nonetheless, the details of his argument may provoke our own engagement with the natural world.

We fervently hope Job is right that there is "hope for a tree" and for all the mountains, lakes, rivers, coral reefs, meadows, and plains gracing our planet. Endangered environments and the creatures inhabiting them deserve a future of abundant life, but that hope cannot be realized without our attention. As we meditate on this passage, we might listen to the trees and hear them delivering a speech not unlike Job's. Like him, they can claim to be innocent sufferers, often failing to direct human action or the impacts of a climate heated by human action. The Book of Job generally raises questions for traditional beliefs in divine justice. This passage raises another question for contemporary readers. What will we do for the trees to have hope?

Harold W. Attridge, PhD
Sterling Professor of Divinity, Emeritus,
at Yale University Divinity School
New Haven, Connecticut

Questions

What are the trees that grow near you? How are they reacting to contemporary challenges of human action, climate change, or invasive species?

What can be done in your environment to give hope to trees and those who love them?

Prayer

O God of heaven and earth, teach us to appreciate the marvels of the world that you have made. Train us to listen to all the voices of innocent sufferers, including those of the plants and animals with which you have filled the earth. Help us to be faithful stewards of your creation. *Amen.*

Job 38:1-21

¹Then the LORD answered Job out of the whirlwind: ²"Who is this that darkens counsel by words without knowledge? ³Gird up your loins like a man, I will question you, and you shall declare to me.

⁴"Where were you when I laid the foundation of the earth? Tell me, if you have understanding. ⁵Who determined its measurements —surely you know! Or who stretched the line upon it? ⁶On what were its bases sunk, or who laid its cornerstone ⁷when the morning stars sang together and all the heavenly beings shouted for joy? ⁸"Or who shut in the sea with doors when it burst out from the womb?—⁹when I made the clouds its garment, and thick darkness its swaddling band, ¹⁰and prescribed bounds for it, and set bars and doors, ¹¹and said, 'Thus far shall you come, and no farther, and here shall your proud waves be stopped'?

¹²"Have you commanded the morning since your days began, and caused the dawn to know its place, ¹³so that it might take hold of the skirts of the earth, and the wicked be shaken out of it? ¹⁴It is changed like clay under the seal, and it is dyed like a garment. ¹⁵Light is withheld from the wicked, and their uplifted arm is broken. ¹⁶"Have you entered into the springs of the sea, or walked in the recesses of the deep? ¹⁷Have the gates of death been revealed to you, or have you seen the gates of deep darkness? ¹⁸Have you comprehended the expanse of the earth? Declare, if you know all this. ¹⁹"Where is the way to the dwelling of light, and where is the place of darkness, ²⁰that you may take it to its territory and that you may discern the paths to its home? ²¹Surely you know, for you were born then, and the number of your days is great!"

Reflection

Amid the atrocities and hardships facing us, it is easy to forget the owner and creator of us all. When problems hit us and solutions seem far-fetched and hard to reach, and our energy is drained, hope is shaken, and our friends accuse us unjustly, it can be easy to forget about the goodness and mightiness of our God. In this passage, we are reminded that God is the owner of the whole universe. God, therefore, knows the best plans that God has for us, even in the face of uncertainties and problems.

God reminds Job about God's mightiness and wonders. God tells him about the mysteries of creation. God gets Job to perceive God's greatness through creation. Indeed, the glory and greatness of God is revealed in the Creator's creation (Psalm 19:1-4). Isn't it amazing that God spoke to Job out of the whirlwind concerning God's wonderful acts of creation of the universe? God uses God's creatures to teach powerful lessons to Job.

Reading the Bible, we see this way of teaching, of using creatures as teaching aids, throughout the entire Bible (see Job 12:7-10; Psalms 96:11-12; 104:24-25; Matthew 13:1-53). In his teachings, Jesus often uses nature to communicate about the Kingdom of God with his audience. Jesus sets for us a perfect example of the importance of nature in the Christian circles when teaching about God and God's character. God owns everything (Deuteronomy 10:14; Psalm 16:2; Romans 11:36), and as such, we can teach by using nature.

Our understanding of the owner of the whole universe should help us to see ourselves as God's stewards. Nature is supposed to be protected and cherished because through it, God reveals God's nature and divine self. Destroying God's creation robs us of this insightful revelation. Whether we are Christians or belong to any other religion, we must all help take good care of creation.

The Rev. Canon Andrew Sumani
Assistant Priest, St. James Parish, Anglican Diocese of Lake Malawi
Principal of the Lake Malawi Anglican University, Malawi
Former Diocesan Environmental Coordinator
Lilongwe, Malawi

Questions

How does our understanding of biblical creation affect the way we relate to nature? Think of any biblical lessons drawn from nature in your context and explain how these lessons can nourish your relationship with God.

How should we care for nature and God's creation? If we have not been faithful in caring for God's creation, what actions will we take from now onward? Please ensure that you draw a workable and implementable plan—and do it!

Prayer

O God, the creator of the heavens and the earth, without you nothing was created. The heavens and the earth belong to you; Grant us your grace, O God, to be able to live a God-fearing life by caring for your creation in a manner that pleases you. We know, O God, that if we work without you, our efforts bear no fruits at all. Therefore, help us to do all things through Christ who strengthen us. This we pray, through Jesus Christ our Lord and Redeemer. *Amen.*

Psalm 8:3-9

³You have set up a stronghold against your adversaries,*
   to quell the enemy and the avenger.

⁴When I consider your heavens, the work of your fingers,*
   the moon and the stars you have set in their courses,

⁵What is man that you should be mindful of him?*
   the son of man that you should seek him out?

⁶You have made him but little lower than the angels;*
   you adorn him with glory and honor;

⁷You give him mastery over the works of your hands;*
   you put all things under his feet:

⁸All sheep and oxen,*
   even the wild beasts of the field,

⁹The birds of the air, the fish of the sea,*
   and whatsoever walks in the paths of the sea.

Reflection

"Attentiveness is the prayer of the soul," said Nicolas Malebranche, a seventeenth-century priest and philosopher. Attentiveness may also be the hope of creation. Psalm 8 speaks of attentiveness, or mindfulness, a theme we hear a lot about these days. By paying attention to the heavens, the psalmist recognizes the miracle of God's mindfulness, the grace that the God of creation pays attention to us at all.

The psalm also invites attentiveness to the beauty of creation, by which we see ourselves as part of creation, not separate from it. The observation of the glories of creation leads to an attitude of gratitude, a profound sense of worship. With that celebration comes responsibility, the granting of dominion, an echo of the responsibility given to Adam and Eve. As in many places in scripture, the psalm asks: What will we do with what we have been given? How will we be stewards of creation?

In our flawed history, the interpretation of dominion has been twisted to imply exploitation, to mean that we can do whatever we wanted with creation for selfish purposes. It's based on the illusion that we are somehow distinct from creation, above it all, so we can use it all, without regard for the loving intention of the Creator, the healing of the world.

For centuries, this could be done to little visible effect. But modern times indicate that our exercise of dominion—the ways we treat air and water, how we exhaust limited resources, the ways we grow and harvest crops or raise animals for our dinner table, and our disregard for other species—are catching up with us.

We are called to a new and holy frame of mind. It may well begin with attentiveness, a mindfulness of the goodness God graciously

The Creation Care Bible Challenge

sets before us. It's all how we look at it. Albert Einstein said that we can look at the world in two ways: as if nothing is a miracle or as if everything is a miracle. May our attentiveness to the miracle of God's mindfulness of us invoke our call to more mindful living and move us to deeper creation care.

The Rev. Jay Sidebotham
Associate for Formation at St. James' Episcopal Church
New York City, New York

Questions _____

How does your attentiveness to creation shape your faith?

What do you learn from looking at the heavens?

When in the rhythm of your week do you find moments of mindfulness about the beauty of creation?

What do you see as your responsibility for creation care in light of this psalm?

Prayer _____

Gracious God, we marvel at your mindfulness toward us, your gracious and loving regard for us as part of the creation you called very good. As we give thanks for all good gifts around us, coming from heaven above, we ask you to make us attentive to the beauty of creation and to take to heart our own responsibility for its care. We pray in the power of the undivided Trinity, eternal majesty, incarnate word and ever-living Spirit. *Amen.*

Psalm 19:1-5

¹The heavens declare the glory of God,*
    and the firmament shows his handiwork.

²One day tells its tale to another,*
    and one night imparts knowledge to another.

³Although they have no words or language,*
    and their voices are not heard,

⁴Their sound has gone out into all lands,*
    and their message to the ends of the world.

⁵In the deep has he set a pavilion for the sun;*
    it comes forth like a bridegroom out of his chamber;
    it rejoices like a champion to run its course.

Reflection

A few years ago, bishops of the Episcopal Church gathered in Alaska. While we were there, a priest of that diocese, an indigenous person, spoke of his people's knowledge of God before they heard the gospel from missionaries of the Episcopal Church. I still ponder what he said: "We knew about the Great Creator because we could see God in the sky, in the forests, in the living things, and in the flowing water. We had the general revelation of God, and you brought us the specific revelation of God in Jesus."

I remember those words whenever I'm looking at the stars in the sky or the light of dawn dancing on the water or listening to the trees moaning in the winds. I think of his words when I watch the seals sunning themselves on the rocks in the winter or the smelts running from a fishing cormorant. These everyday wonders fill my heart with awe. They spark my imagination and make me reflect on their origins and their interconnections. They bring me closer to God, their Creator.

None of these things speak words I can hear, yet they eloquently proclaim a message that inspires and instructs me. When the psalmist says the "heavens declare" and that "their voice goes to the ends of the world," I believe I understand the point. Often the most profound teaching comes not with words but through embodiment. I can read and write about the wonder of creation, but when I experience it firsthand, I am entering into the heart of God's realm.

We can learn about God's particular desires for us by studying and praying about Jesus's teaching and his example. But we can learn about God too by studying and reflecting on the surprising beauty and design of the everyday events of nature. Being stewards of the creation isn't simply our duty; it protects one of our primary sources of divine revelation.

The Rt. Rev. Nicholas Knisely
Bishop of the Diocese of Rhode Island
Providence, Rhode Island

Questions

When did you see something in nature that filled you with awe? Have you thanked God spontaneously because you had that moment?

Do you better understand God's creative work because of what you have experienced in the natural world?

Prayer

Holy One, Creator of the sun and the stars, the rainclouds and rainbow, and all the wonders of the physical world, give us curiosity about you and call us to seek a deeper understanding of you by studying nature. Inspire us to share what we have learned so that our neighbors will, in turn, seek you. In all these things help us to preserve what we encounter so that our children might know you, too. In Jesus's Name we ask this. *Amen.*

Psalm 24:1-3

[1]The earth is the LORD's and all that is in it,*
   the world and all who dwell therein.

[2]For it is he who founded it upon the seas*
   and made it firm upon the rivers of the deep.

[3]"Who can ascend the hill of the LORD?*
   And who can stand in his holy place?"

Reflection

Seeing a kingfisher is normally a fleeting flash of vivid blue as the bird disappears along the stream. This kingfisher was different: we were walking through Bibury, in the English Cotswolds where we live, and saw the kingfisher sitting on a wall. He was so still that we could photograph him. People were going past, but he seemed pretty oblivious of them. He belonged to Bibury, this was his river, and he was on the hunt to make at least one fish his lunch!

Psalm 24 explains that the earth belongs to God and all that is in it. The Hebrew word for that last phrase is *melo*. It is sometimes translated as fullness. All the richness of biodiversity in the earth belongs to God. But they do not only belong to God: he has also given them a dwelling place, a home where they live. My small kingfisher knew where he belonged, and that belonging multiplied billions of times is the fullness of the earth that God has made.

We read in Colossians 1:19-20 that God's fullness is in Christ, who redeemed and reconciled all things through his blood shed on the cross. As we look in wonder at the fullness of the earth, let us not forget that it belongs to the Lord. May we have a fresh understanding of Christ who reconciles all things, including kingfishers, and work to restore the fullness that has been stripped away by our greed and carelessness.

The Rev. Margot R. Hodson
Director of Theology and Education at the John Ray Initiative
Oxfordshire, England

Questions

How does understanding nature as God's fullness broaden our understanding of the tasks of Christian discipleship?

If God has made all things, then stripping the earth of its fullness is sin. How can we confess this appropriately?

Psalm 24:4 says those with clean hands and pure hearts shall ascend the hill of the Lord. How can we change our hearts and hands to live in a way that seeks to be life-giving to all (human and non-human) inhabitants of the earth?

Prayer

Lord, we marvel at the vivid tapestry of creatures that fly, swim, run, and walk on the earth. We are thankful for the beauty of plants from the tallest of trees to the tiniest of flowers. Yet, we grieve that our lifestyles have been stripping the earth of its God-given fullness. Give us courage to live our lives differently as disciples of Christ who reconciles all things through his blood shed on the cross. *Amen.*

Psalm 95:1-11

¹Come, let us sing to the LORD;*
    let us shout for joy to the Rock of our salvation.

²Let us come before his presence with thanksgiving*
    and raise a loud shout to him with psalms.

³For the LORD is a great God, and a great King above all gods.

⁴In his hand are the caverns of the earth,*
    and the heights of the hills are his also.

⁵The sea is his, for he made it,*
    and his hands have molded the dry land.

⁶Come, let us bow down, and bend the knee,*
    and kneel before the LORD our Maker.

⁷For he is our God, and we are the people of his pasture and the
        sheep of his hand.*
    Oh, that today you would hearken to his voice!

⁸Harden not your hearts, as your forebears did in the wilderness,*
    at Meribah, and on that day at Massah, when they tempted me.

⁹They put me to the test,*
    though they had seen my works.

¹⁰Forty years long I detested that generation and said,*
    "This people are wayward in their hearts; they do not know my ways."

¹¹So I swore in my wrath,*
    "They shall not enter into my rest."

Reflection

"When I started surfing at age nineteen, I stopped going to church." My seventy-five-year-old friend Gramps told me this at his board repair shop in Haiku, Maui. We both knew exactly what he meant. "The sea is his, for he made it." A mysterious encounter with the Creator draws us into the ocean, where we experience indescribable joy. On the edge of that vast sea, we feel the pulse of the planet, the energy of storms thousands of miles away. We also face danger, forces that could kill us.

Moments of transcendence in God's creation speak to our soul. It could be a meadow of poppies and lupines on a California spring day, or the way light filters through a cathedral of redwood trees, or in the impossibly clear water as you race down the face of a wave over schools of tropical fish, or the nighttime constellation of stars called Maui's Fishhook.

Twenty-five hundred years ago, the author of Psalm 95 understood how awe confronts us in creation and invited us to "sing to the Lord… to shout for joy to the Rock of our salvation." At the same time, this person also recognized how easy it is for us to be blind to the beauty of creation.

The author goes as far as to imagine what this ingratitude looks like from God's perspective. The psalmist feels indignant that the people of God, fleeing slavery through Meribah and Massah, feel such a great thirst that they threaten the life of Moses and abandon God.

As a child, I memorized Psalm 95 by hearing it repeated in Sunday Morning Prayer. It still helps me. I'm glad I was in church and not out surfing.

We all miss what is being given to us. We thirst. Psalms like this remind us that we can bring our whole selves to God. The psalms gave Jesus, Mary, Peter, and Paul a language to understand how God was connected to their own experience. Put these words into your heart and rejoice.

The Very Rev. Malcolm Clemens Young
Dean of Grace Cathedral
San Francisco, California

Questions

Where do you encounter God's beauty? What thirst draws you away from the experience of gratitude?

How does your imagination of what could be lead you to fail to appreciate what is?

Prayer

O Holy Creator, you put in our hearts such a love for the vast expanses of creation, for places where we see the work of your hand and rejoice. Bring us, your wayward children, home so that we may sing psalms of thanksgiving and know you more perfectly. We pray this in the Name of the one who seeks us, the Good Shepherd, Jesus Christ our Lord. *Amen.*

Psalm 104:10-32

¹⁰You send the springs into the valleys;*
    they flow between the mountains.

¹¹All the beasts of the field drink their fill from them,*
    and the wild asses quench their thirst.

¹²Beside them the birds of the air make their nests*
    and sing among the branches.

¹³You water the mountains from your dwelling on high;*
    the earth is fully satisfied by the fruit of your works.

¹⁴You make grass grow for flocks and herds*
    and plants to serve mankind;

¹⁵That they may bring forth food from the earth,*
    and wine to gladden our hearts,

¹⁶Oil to make a cheerful countenance,*
    and bread to strengthen the heart.

¹⁷The trees of the LORD are full of sap,*
    the cedars of Lebanon which he planted,

¹⁸In which the birds build their nests,*
    and in whose tops the stork makes his dwelling.

¹⁹The high hills are a refuge for the mountain goats,*
    and the stony cliffs for the rock badgers.

²⁰You appointed the moon to mark the seasons,*
    and the sun knows the time of its setting.

²¹You make darkness that it may be night,*
    in which all the beasts of the forest prowl.

²²The lions roar after their prey*
    and seek their food from God.

²³The sun rises, and they slip away*
    and lay themselves down in their dens.

²⁴Man goes forth to his work*
    and to his labor until the evening.

²⁵O LORD, how manifold are your works!*
    In wisdom you have made them all; the earth is
        full of your creatures.

²⁶Yonder is the great and wide sea with its living things too many to
        number,*
    creatures both small and great.

²⁷There move the ships, and there is that Leviathan,*
    which you have made for the sport of it.

²⁸All of them look to you*
    to give them their food in due season.

²⁹You give it to them; they gather it;*
    you open your hand, and they are filled with good things.

³⁰You hide your face, and they are terrified;*
    you take away their breath, and they die and return to their dust.

³¹You send forth your Spirit, and they are created;*
    and so you renew the face of the earth.

³²May the glory of the LORD endure for ever;*
    may the LORD rejoice in all his works.

Reflection

"Lost in wonder, love, and praise." These are the closing words of Charles Wesley's hymn, "Love Divine, All Loves Excelling." They can also serve as a summary of Psalm 104 and its celebration of God's majestic creation.

Wonder is not a word we routinely use to describe our experience of the natural world around us, any more than its synonym awe. There are occasions, however, when only those words will suffice.

It was 5 a.m. on the south rim of the Grand Canyon. We were waiting for the sun to rise. Nobody spoke in more than a whisper. Then a bunch of noisy teenagers burst upon the scene. When they saw the canyon, they stopped dead in their tracks. Possibly for the first time in their lives, they were encountering something that filled them with wonder. For once, "awesome" would have been an appropriate response!

Imagine the psalmist sitting high up on a hillside, letting his eyes take in all the dimensions of life laid out before him. Filled with wonder, he cries out: "O Lord, how manifold are your works! In wisdom you have made them all."

Love undergirds all the creation that God has made. When we pray, "Give us this day our daily bread," we know that we can trust our loving Father to provide for our needs. The psalmist reminds us that all the manifold works of God are similarly sustained: "All of them look to you to give them their food in due season." Life and death alike belong to God, and the loving work of creation goes forward.

Praise belongs on our lips as the appropriate response to the wonders of creation and the love that is God's daily gift to us all. As the psalm continues in verse 34, "I will sing to the Lord as long as I live; I will praise my God while I have my being."

The Rt. Rev. Jeffery Rowthorn
Hymn writer and hymnal editor
Retired Suffragan Bishop of Connecticut and Bishop of Europe
Salem, Connecticut

Questions

Like the teenagers at the Grand Canyon, have you ever been stopped in your tracks and filled with wonder? If so, what caused this response and where were you at the time?

Does "Give us this day our daily bread" apply to more than human beings?

How do you stay close to nature (e.g., photography, painting, hiking/ biking, gardening etc.)?

Prayer

We thank you, Lord our God, for the magnificence of creation, for the smallest atom and the most distant galaxy, for prophets and poets, scientists and musicians. As we open our hands to receive our daily bread, may our eyes and our minds be open to discern your presence in the world around us. Send your Spirit among us and renew the face of the earth. This we ask in Jesus's Name. *Amen.*

Psalm 121

¹I lift up my eyes to the hills*
    from where is my help come?

²My help comes from the LORD,*
    the maker of heaven and earth.

³He will not let your foot be moved;*
    and he who watches over you will not fall asleep.

⁴Behold, he who keeps watch over Israel*
    shall neither slumber nor sleep;

⁵The LORD himself watches over you;*
    the LORD is your shade at your right hand.

⁶So that the sun shall not strike you by day,*
    nor the moon by night.

⁷The LORD shall preserve you from all evil;*
    it is he who shall keep you safe.

⁸The LORD shall watch over your going out and your coming in,*
    from this time forth for evermore.

Reflection

I am about to set out on yet another pilgrimage. This time, I will be hiking the Camino Primitivo. It is the oldest and most difficult—and reportedly the most beautiful—of the twenty-six caminos or routes crisscrossing Spain and leading to Santiago de Compostela. The remains of Saint James the Great, known in Spanish as "Santiago," lie buried inside this stunning cathedral.

Santiago was one of Jesus's twelve disciples. According to tradition, after Jesus's crucifixion, he came to Spain to share the Christian faith. Upon his return to Judea, tradition recalls that he was beheaded by King Herod Agrippa I in 44 CE. His disciples remembered his love for Spain and transported his body in a boat back to Spain, where he was buried in a grave that was lost until a hermit discovered it under a field of stars. Hence, the location is called Santiago de Compostela, the latter meaning "field of stars."

Pilgrims now journey from across the world to hike the Camino Francés, the Camino del Norte, the Camino Portugués, and other lesser-known trails leading to Santiago. They encounter God in nature as they trek. They follow in the footsteps of pilgrims, including King Alfonsus II, who in the ninth century walked from Oviedo to Santiago de Compostela to beseech Santiago for spiritual favors. Pilgrims on the Camino Primitivo retrace his steps.

There is something about "lifting our eyes to the hills" that lifts our spirits, puts life in perspective, makes us realize how small we are and how manageable our problems are, and reminds us of the greatness and majesty of our Creator. Walking slows us down so that we take note of the beauty and wonder of creation. We must travel lightly. So, we simplify our lives as we traverse the mountains, causing us to take stock of what truly matters in life and how we must care for God's glorious creation.

The Rev. Marek P. Zabriskie
Rector of Christ Church and Founder of The Bible Challenge
Greenwich, Connecticut

Questions

Where have you experienced God in the vast outdoors?

Where do you feel closer to God: in the mountains or on the coastline or in some other natural setting?

If you have been able to hike in the mountains, what have your experiences been? What did it make you feel or think?

Prayer

God of all majesty, power, and good, the landscape of creation reveals so much of what we need to know about you, teaching lessons that we must constantly learn and relearn. Inspire us to travel lightly across the earth until we return to the dust from which we were made. Remind us to be faithful stewards of creation, bequeathing to our children, grandchildren, and others the enduring gift of a sustainable planet, but only if we remember that we are stewards, not owners, of this precious earth, our island home. *Amen.*

Psalm 148:5-14

⁵Let them praise the Name of the LORD,*
    for he commanded, and they were created.

⁶He made them stand fast for ever and ever;*
    he gave them a law which shall not pass away.

⁷Praise the LORD from the earth,*
    you sea-monsters and all deeps;

⁸Fire and hail, snow and fog,*
    tempestuous wind doing his will.

⁹Mountains and all hills,*
    fruit trees and all cedars;

¹⁰Wild beasts and all cattle,*
    creeping things and winged birds;

¹¹Kings of the earth and all peoples,*
    princes and all rulers of the world;

¹²Young men and maidens,*
    old and young together.

¹³Let them praise the Name of the LORD,*
    for his Name only is exalted; his splendor is
       over earth and heaven.

¹⁴He has raised up strength for his people, praise for all his loyal servants,*
    the children of Israel, a people who are near him. Hallelujah!

Reflection

The author of Psalm 148 proclaims, "Let them praise the Name of the Lord, for he commanded, and they were created." and "Mountains and all hills, fruit trees and all cedars; Wild beasts and all cattle, creeping things and all winged birds." The psalmist believes that God's splendor is over earth and heaven. God's glorious creation is a marvelous gift.

As part of our baptismal covenant, we commit to seek and serve Christ in all persons, loving our neighbors as ourselves. Neighbor extends beyond our human neighbors, young and old alike, to all of creation. God calls upon us to show love and respect to all and to be faithful stewards of the glorious creation entrusted to us. Loving our neighbors means serving them from the heart with kindness, compassion, and empathy.

Each of us has a responsibility to provide a more sustainable future for generations to come. If we are careless in our stewardship of God's creation and fail to reduce our environmental footprint, we will destroy the splendid variety of species in the ocean, on the land, and in the air. We will harm the vegetation that nourishes and sustains us. Through our indifference or neglect, we may also deny others the opportunity to experience the majesty and blessings of God's creation. Extinction is forever, and causing it is a mournful burden that we need not carry.

It is essential to harmonize the fulfillment of the needs of all creatures through acts of service. Such service could take the form of helping underprivileged children, the elderly, or the homeless, tending a garden patch, planting a tree, advocating for conservation, instituting policy change, or reducing our consumption and waste. It is up to each of us to make creation-care choices and to lead sustainable lifestyles so that our children and grandchildren can enjoy God's magnificently created order and the inspiration and wonder of nature.

Jane L. Snowdon, PhD, FAMIA
Deputy Chief Science Officer of Scientific Operations
at IBM Watson Health
Greenwich, Connecticut

Questions

In what ways are you praising God for creation?

What do you do to promote sustainability and care for God's creation at home within your family?

How might you use your gifts to take even greater action to care for God's creation?

Prayer

Gracious and loving God, we give thanks for the sun, moon, stars, and our wondrous earthly home. Grant us your grace to take time to marvel at and care for the splendor of your creation, from all living creatures in the water, on land, and in the air to the abundance of vegetation that nourishes and sustains us. Create in us a renewed commitment to the care of your creation and glorious gifts. *Amen.*

Proverbs 8:22-36

[22]The Lord created me at the beginning of his work, the first of his acts of long ago. [23]Ages ago I was set up, at the first, before the beginning of the earth. [24]When there were no depths I was brought forth, when there were no springs abounding with water. [25]Before the mountains had been shaped, before the hills, I was brought forth—[26]when he had not yet made earth and fields, or the world's first bits of soil. [27]When he established the heavens, I was there, when he drew a circle on the face of the deep, [28]when he made firm the skies above, when he established the fountains of the deep, [29]when he assigned to the sea its limit, so that the waters might not transgress his command, when he marked out the foundations of the earth, [30]then I was beside him, like a master worker; and I was daily his delight, rejoicing before him always, [31]rejoicing in his inhabited world and delighting in the human race. [32]"And now, my children, listen to me: happy are those who keep my ways. [33]Hear instruction and be wise, and do not neglect it. [34]Happy is the one who listens to me, watching daily at my gates, waiting beside my doors. [35]For whoever finds me finds life and obtains favor from the Lord; [36]but those who miss me injure themselves; all who hate me love death.

Reflection

We live in a time when climate impacts have begun, yet we are still pursuing the activities that are causing them; it can seem as if humanity is unfit for Earth because we are possessed by an illusion that we are separate and superior. For those of us steeped in a biblical worldview and aware of its vast influence, it is tempting to locate the problem right in its creation story. Most of us learned that a male God singlehandedly manifested the whole web of life and then gave the reigns to those made in his image.

This may help explain the strange value system that is blind to the agency of Earth. Most societies assess value according to metrics like the gross domestic product (GDP), which does not count the very things that harm and trigger the biosphere. This includes pollution, depletion, and policies and norms that encourage gross overconsumption and waste by some while tolerating deprivation for others. Some even suggest we take a chance on geoengineering the sky in an attempt to accommodate all this, a version of "playing God," if there ever was one. More than new technology, we need ancient wisdom.

In Proverbs 8, Wisdom is not merely an abstraction. She is a force present since "before the beginning of the earth." Her intimacy with God is key to creation: "I was beside him like a master worker, and I was his daily delight." She loves humans but tells us to behave wisely or perish: "And now my children, listen to me: happy are those who keep my ways…those who miss me injure themselves; all who hate me love death."

This voice is an invitation to restore balance and belonging. Creation is more than a material world handed down to us as a gift; it encompasses the laws of nature, including gravity, the carbon cycle, procreation, and the dynamics of water, air, soil, and fire. As we do the work of creation care, we often encounter confusion, despair, and false solutions. Wisdom tells us to watch at her gates and wait by her doors.

Karenna Gore
Founder and Executive Director of the
Center for Earth Ethics at Union Theological Seminary
New York City, New York

Questions

What does it mean to listen to Wisdom? Where are her gates and doors?

How does this account change your understanding of the biblical creation story in the book of Genesis, if at all?

Prayer

Creator, we pray with gratitude for the wisdom in creation, for the way laws of nature provide for our protection and learning. We pray to perceive the gates and doors through which we receive guidance to live in balance and harmony within this beautiful web of life. *Amen.*

Ecclesiastes 3:1-3

¹For everything there is a season, and a time for every matter under heaven: ²a time to be born, and a time to die; a time to plant, and a time to pluck up what is planted; ³a time to kill, and a time to heal; a time to break down, and a time to build up.

Reflection

This Bible passage has always been a favorite of mine, especially the first verse. As I read it, I imagine the unfolding of nature during the year. I live in a climate with four distinct seasons. The quiet, cold of winter is followed in due time by the exuberance of spring growth. The full greenness of summer with leafy trees and plentiful flowers melds into the autumnal harvest season. The year rotates back to winter.

As you read these passages, think about the series of opposites and what the writer is trying to get us to think about. The words encourage us to think about the world around us as well as our way of life. Many of us live lives far removed from the way of life described in this passage. We are not required to raise our own food to feed our families; we are not in tune with the cycles of planting and harvesting. For our ancestors, knowing about the seasonal nature of foods and how and where to find them was an integral part of their lives.

I am so lucky that I am a gardener, which connects me directly to the earth and its seasons. If I don't plant my peas on the right day, they will not germinate, and I will not be able to pluck them and eat them. The writer uses this metaphor for all of our earthly activities, but it can also call us to get back in touch with a seasonal growing life.

Think carefully about your own life at the moment and how the scripture applies to it. "For everything there is a season" is a powerful statement that needs some thought. For me, the words remind me to live my life in the moment, taking in the sensory joys of my garden, walks in nature, and thanking God for all of my blessings.

Jenny Rose Carey
Renowned gardener, educator, public speaker,
and author of several gardening books
Ambler, Pennsylvania

Questions

How can I become more aware of the seasonal nature of life and think about its impact on my own life? Some possibilities include taking walks in nature or volunteering at a local nature preserve or garden.

How can I change habits in my life to be more in touch with the fruits and vegetables in season?

What can I find in the natural world to be thankful for today?

Prayer

Dear Lord, please help me to be aware of the cycles of nature in the world around me. Help me rediscover a connection to the land that I live in and relish the beauty of my local environment. Help me find peace in nature and be grateful for the gifts that you have given us. *Amen.*

Isaiah 24:5-6

5The earth lies polluted under its inhabitants; for they have transgressed laws, violated the statutes, broken the everlasting covenant. 6Therefore a curse devours the earth, and its inhabitants suffer for their guilt; therefore the inhabitants of the earth dwindled, and few people are left.

Reflection

According to the prophet Isaiah, the ritual and ethical corruptions of his society were endangering the entire created order. He believed faithlessness to the Torah was leading to the very undoing of nature. He was not alone in this view, with similar pronouncements by the prophets Hosea (4:1-3) and Jeremiah (4:23-26).

It was Iron Age thinking that led the prophets to assume a direct causality between ethical trespasses by humans and the suffering of the natural, geological world. But that link is now based on scientific thinking.

In a pre-scientific world, the religious geniuses of ancient Israel that we know as the Hebrew prophets captured a truth through intuitive folk wisdom: the prophetic insistence that human misbehavior initiates a cycle of chaos and destruction that devastates the social and natural worlds. Their call to faithfulness to the everlasting convent of mutuality among all life forms was never timelier.

The Rev. Dr. Gregory Mobley
Professor of Hebrew Bible at Yale Divinity School
New Haven, Connecticut

Questions

How has human behavior polluted and devoured the earth?

What are some practical steps we can take individually and collectively to repent for these trespasses so that these curses might be supplanted by blessings?

Prayer

Lord, make us instruments of thy *shalom*, living in ways that support the unity and beauty of all life on earth. *Amen.*

Jeremiah 2:9-17

⁹Therefore once more I accuse you, says the Lord, and I accuse your children's children. ¹⁰Cross to the coasts of Cyprus and look, send to Kedar and examine with care; see if there has ever been such a thing. ¹¹Has a nation changed its gods, even though they are no gods? But my people have changed their glory for something that does not profit. ¹²Be appalled, O heavens, at this, be shocked, be utterly desolate, says the Lord, ¹³for my people have committed two evils: they have forsaken me, the fountain of living water, and dug out cisterns for themselves, cracked cisterns that can hold no water.

¹⁴Is Israel a slave? Is he a homeborn servant? Why then has he become plunder? ¹⁵The lions have roared against him, they have roared loudly. They have made his land a waste; his cities are in ruins, without inhabitant. ¹⁶Moreover, the people of Memphis and Tahpanhes have broken the crown of your head. ¹⁷Have you not brought this upon yourself by forsaking the Lord your God, while he led you in the way?

Reflection

The message of the biblical prophet Jeremiah still has a bearing on our lives today. Jeremiah is one of those prophets who spoke his mind with much tenacity—and without fear or favor. His message challenges those in authority as well as the people of Judah to come out of their comfort zone and face the reality that Yahweh is angry.

Israel and Judah have deviated from the covenant that Yahweh made with their forefathers. In his message, Jeremiah reminds his adherents of the imminent threat before them. Jeremiah, in his prophecies, is upholding the Mosaic Tradition and calling upon Judah not to make the same mistake that had been made before. For the first time in Jeremiah 2:15b, the prophet does not use a metaphor. He makes it known how Judah has perverted the land into a desert and how the cities are in ruins.

The same can be said of how humanity has failed to be God's ordained stewards in safeguarding the environment and preserving the natural beauty of creation. Earth is bleeding and in dire need of preservation. Humanity has not done much to preserve and safeguard the natural inhabitants of Mother Earth. The planet is experiencing severe droughts, flooding, heat waves, rising sea level, and melting of glaciers among other disasters. Whilst on the other hand, humanity is debating in conferences and summits about whether climate change is a reality or who is more responsible for the emission of greenhouse gases in the atmosphere.

There are many passages in both the Old and New Testaments that speak about creation care and how humans should act as agents for safeguarding the created order.

There are enough charges and reasons for humanity to create a new mindset and drive to give Mother Earth our utmost attention.

The Rev. Masango Roderick Warakula
Lecturer at National Anglican Theological College of Zimbabwe
Harare, Zimbabwe

Questions

Which actions should we take to make planet Earth safe and habitable?

Why is the current global environmental degradation not challenging humanity to act?

Can issues of environmental justice and climate change be separated from our spiritual lives and welfare?

Prayer

Merciful and gracious God, you have made us your stewards to look after that which you have created. Pour into our hearts such love to do what is just and give us the courage to safeguard the beauty of your creation. Direct our hearts to your constant love and make our actions celebrate your goodness. *Amen.*

Jeremiah 29:4-14

4Thus says the LORD of hosts, the God of Israel, to all the exiles whom I have sent into exile from Jerusalem to Babylon: 5Build houses and live in them; plant gardens and eat what they produce. 6Take wives and have sons and daughters; take wives for your sons, and give your daughters in marriage, that they may bear sons and daughters; multiply there, and do not decrease. 7But seek the welfare of the city where I have sent you into exile, and pray to the LORD on its behalf, for in its welfare you will find your welfare. 8For thus says the LORD of hosts, the God of Israel: Do not let the prophets and the diviners who are among you deceive you, and do not listen to the dreams that they dream, 9for it is a lie that they are prophesying to you in my name; I did not send them, says the LORD.

10For thus says the LORD: Only when Babylon's seventy years are completed will I visit you, and I will fulfill to you my promise and bring you back to this place. 11For surely I know the plans I have for you, says the LORD, plans for your welfare and not for harm, to give you a future with hope. 12Then when you call upon me and come and pray to me, I will hear you. 13When you search for me, you will find me; if you seek me with all your heart, 14I will let you find me, says the LORD, and I will restore your fortunes and gather you from all the nations and all the places where I have driven you, says the LORD, and I will bring you back to the place from which I sent you into exile.

Reflection

Build houses and live in them; plant gardens and eat what they produce.
These are a few of the instructions God gives the people of Israel while
they are living in exile in Babylon. These instructions don't seem to be
intended for a temporary stay.

I grew up in a faith tradition that placed a lot of emphasis on the next
life—the one that comes after this earth, after these bodies. Songs,
catchphrases, platitudes, Bible studies, sermons—all our language
was centered on "getting to" or "being in" heaven. The earth, (and
by extension all the things of earth, including bodies, soil, trees, and
oceans) were seen as temporary, and therefore the care of them (in any
meaningful way) was optional.

There are a lot of problems with this way of thinking. If heaven is the
point, why do we know so little about it? Why are there so many more
instructions in the Bible for how to love and care for creation—from
our neighbor's pig to our neighboring human? If heaven is the point,
why talk about earthly things at all? And why would Jesus take on
flesh, break bread, drink wine, draw in the sand, and walk on the
water? Why bother?

In Jeremiah 29:4-14, we see God giving some straightforward and
practical instructions to the Hebrew people. They are not where they
want to be—stuck in Babylon, far from the home they long for, the
place they exult. But Babylon is where they are and putting down
roots is what God tells them to do. Build houses, God says. Don't
just pitch temporary tents; build permanent structures. Plant gardens.
And not just any gardens: don't try and plant what you grew in Israel;
plant what will grow in this soil, the soil that you have, not the soil
you wish you had. Do all the things needed to flourish where you are,

do all the things needed to care for the place where you are planted, and stop living for what might be someday.

When I think of what it means to love God, to love what God loves, this is the passage I always come back to. This is the passage that challenges me to be intentional about how I live on this earth and care for all my neighbors, two-legged, four-legged, elemental, and atmospheric.

Jerusalem Jackson Greer
Staff Officer for Evangelism, The Episcopal Church
Greenbrier, Arkansas

Questions

How would it change your perspective to begin to think of all of creation as your neighbor (neighbor water, neighbor honeybee, neighbor soil, etc.)?

Are you living a temporary existence, waiting for a "someday" change before you cultivate and care for the place where you are? How can you put down roots of intention?

Prayer

Creator God, help us be present to the life that we have, to the world you have given us, and to all manner of our neighbors around us, as we learn to care for what we have instead of waiting for what might be. Help us to love as you love, right where we are. May we grow deep roots of gratefulness that will sustain us as we seek to care for our neighbor earth and all her inhabitants, including ourselves and our spaces. In the name of Jesus, who came in the flesh, to this earth. *Amen.*

Ezekiel 12:17-28

¹⁷The word of the LORD came to me: ¹⁸Mortal, eat your bread with quaking, and drink your water with trembling and with fearfulness; ¹⁹and say to the people of the land, Thus says the Lord GOD concerning the inhabitants of Jerusalem in the land of Israel: They shall eat their bread with fearfulness, and drink their water in dismay, because their land shall be stripped of all it contains, on account of the violence of all those who live in it. ²⁰The inhabited cities shall be laid waste, and the land shall become a desolation; and you shall know that I am the LORD.

²¹The word of the LORD came to me: ²²Mortal, what is this proverb of yours about the land of Israel, which says, "The days are prolonged, and every vision comes to nothing"? ²³Tell them therefore, "Thus says the Lord GOD: I will put an end to this proverb, and they shall use it no more as a proverb in Israel." But say to them, The days are near, and the fulfillment of every vision. ²⁴For there shall no longer be any false vision or flattering divination within the house of Israel. ²⁵But I the LORD will speak the word that I speak, and it will be fulfilled. It will no longer be delayed; but in your days, O rebellious house, I will speak the word and fulfill it, says the Lord GOD. ²⁶The word of the LORD came to me: ²⁷Mortal, the house of Israel is saying, "The vision that he sees is for many years ahead; he prophesies for distant times." ²⁸Therefore say to them, Thus says the Lord GOD: None of my words will be delayed any longer, but the word that I speak will be fulfilled, says the Lord GOD.

Reflection

When we think of caring for God's creation, many of us are motivated by beautiful mountain vistas with clear rivers running through pristine wilderness. We almost never think of rot, decay, and death. Yet these are essential parts of God's cycle of renewal for our planet. An important part of our spiritual practice of creation care is to acknowledge rot and decay and to see God's love and restoration moving through them.

Just as Jesus entered the hard work of salvation for us through the gateway of death, so do we practice claiming God wherever we are in the creation cycle, especially when we are in death and destruction. When you see the beautiful sunset, be sure to praise rot and decay, which helps us reclaim and clean our water, treat our refuse, and even enjoy fellowship with wine on our tables. Indeed, our Eucharist feast depends on the noble rot and decay of the grape.

Praise God with your actions as you enter all aspects of the creation cycle, including rot and decay. Remember God when you recycle your trash. Let this be a thank offering as you pray. Save table scraps and place them in your garden or potted plants. Live with the mystery of regeneration that comes when we embrace God's cycle of compassion that passes through death to new life.

Praise God with confidence even when disaster strikes. Regret the pain and suffering but boldly claim that, even in the most desolate areas on earth, places like Chernobyl or Fukushima, God's regenerative love is working to break down the toxins and restore creation to balance. Marvel at the plants and animals reclaiming God's creation for life: life that comes out of horrible death and destruction.

Pray in these ways. Then you can clear the high spiritual bar set by Ezekiel, "The inhabited cities shall be laid waste, and the land shall become a desolation and you shall know that I am the Lord."

The Rev. Bill Lupfer
Priest-in-Charge at Christ Church
Aspen, Colorado

Questions

When you drink water, do you think about how that water is very, very old and has washed countless diseased, decaying, and dying ancestors, including Jesus? How can you drink water in a prayerful way that encourages you to embrace the totality of the creation cycle?

Can you prayerfully collect table food scraps and use them to fertilize your garden or potted plants?

Would you consider visiting a decaying, desolate, dying place and ask how God is calling you to respond?

Prayer

Creator of the Universe, you love us so much that nothing is outside of your saving embrace. Strengthen our imagination to see you everywhere and give us spiritual power to join you in the renewing of your creation, especially in places that are desolate, broken, rotten, and dying. For you, O Creator, surround us with your love and strengthen our lives for the renewing of your creation. *Amen*.

Ezekiel 47:6-12

⁶He said to me, "Mortal, have you seen this?" Then he led me back along the bank of the river. ⁷As I came back, I saw on the bank of the river a great many trees on the one side and on the other. ⁸He said to me, "This water flows toward the eastern region and goes down into the Arabah; and when it enters the sea, the sea of stagnant waters, the water will become fresh. ⁹Wherever the river goes, every living creature that swarms will live, and there will be very many fish, once these waters reach there. It will become fresh; and everything will live where the river goes. ¹⁰People will stand fishing beside the sea from En-gedi to En-eglaim; it will be a place for the spreading of nets; its fish will be of a great many kinds, like the fish of the Great Sea. ¹¹But its swamps and marshes will not become fresh; they are to be left for salt. ¹²On the banks, on both sides of the river, there will grow all kinds of trees for food. Their leaves will not wither nor their fruit fail, but they will bear fresh fruit every month, because the water for them flows from the sanctuary. Their fruit will be for food, and their leaves for healing."

Reflection

Despite being about ten times as salty as the oceans, the Dead Sea is not actually dead. Microscopic algae and bacteria thrive in this inhospitable environment, but fish and other larger organisms cannot. En-gedi and En-eglaim are both on the shore of the Dead Sea, but our passage from Ezekiel has it teeming with fish of many kinds, with fishermen along the banks. A river is depicted as flowing down into the Arabah where the Dead Sea is located, and the sea's waters turn from highly saline to fresh. Everywhere the river flows, new life springs up.

The New Testament continues this theme. The famous post-resurrection passage in John 21:1-14 has the disciples fishing on the Sea of Galilee. They are not successful until Jesus tells them to throw their net on the other side of the boat, and a huge catch of 153 fish is netted. The new creation is breaking through into the old. Some have suggested that 153 is a pointer, using a complex Hebrew numerological system known as *gematria*, to both En-gedi and En-eglaim. But whether or not this is the case, both Ezekiel and John describe fish being caught where they would not be expected: one, in the highly saline Dead Sea; the other, just by switching the position of the nets after a very unsuccessful night of fishing.

In Revelation 22:2, the passage refers to Ezekiel with a vast river flowing down from Jerusalem, and the "leaves of the tree are for the healing of the nations." All of these texts are beautiful illustrations of a renewed and restored creation at the end of the age.

Dr. Martin J. Hodson
Operations Director for the John Ray Initiative
Oxfordshire, England

Questions

You may like to investigate the link between 153 and En-gedi and En-eglaim. It is an interesting story!

What are the common features of Ezekiel 47:6-12, John 21:1-14, and Revelation 22:2?

What does a renewed creation look like? How can we live our lives so that we are helping to renew and restore our wounded creation?

Prayer

Dear Lord, we thank you for your wonderful creation. We are truly sorry that we have made such a mess of it; climate change, biodiversity loss, and soil degradation are just three of the symptoms of our environmental crisis. We are grateful that throughout the Bible, we can see glimpses of your wonderful plan for the renewal and restoration of creation. Show us how we can do better and how we can help. *Amen.*

Hosea 2:18-23

[18]I will make for you a covenant on that day with the wild animals, the birds of the air, and the creeping things of the ground; and I will abolish the bow, the sword, and war from the land; and I will make you lie down in safety. [19]And I will take you for my wife forever; I will take you for my wife in righteousness and in justice, in steadfast love, and in mercy. [20]I will take you for my wife in faithfulness; and you shall know the LORD.

[21]On that day I will answer, says the LORD, I will answer the heavens and they shall answer the earth; [22]and the earth shall answer the grain, the wine, and the oil, and they shall answer Jezreel; [23]and I will sow him for myself in the land. And I will have pity on Lo-ruhamah, and I will say to Lo-ammi, "You are my people"; and he shall say, "You are my God."

Reflection

The prophet Hosea reminds us that God made "a covenant on that day with the wild animals, the birds of the air, and the creeping things on the ground" (Hosea 2:18). We humans tend to think that it's all about us, that God cares chiefly about us. That's hardly the case. While we are vital, so are the hummingbirds that dip and dart and the bees that pollinate our gardens. All of them are equally precious to God, and if we don't come to grips with this, our planet will be in peril.

Of all the animals on earth, few are more captivating than the hummingbird. It is a joy to watch them perform their aerial maneuvers. In his book, *One Long River of Song*, Brian Doyle notes that the hummingbird's heart is the size of an eraser. It beats ten times per second. The first explorers to visit the Americas called them *joyas voladoras* or flying jewels, for hummingbirds were found only in the Americas. Today, more than 300 species hum, zip, and zoom.

Each hummingbird visits 1,000 flowers a day. They can dive at 60 miles an hour as well as fly backward. A hummingbird can fly for 500 miles without pausing to rest.

Doyle notes that when hummingbirds rest, they come close to death, especially on frigid nights or when they are starving. Their racecar-like hearts nearly come to a halt, barely beating their wings. If they do not soon find something sweet, their hearts will soon grow cold, and they will cease to be. What would life be without the hummingbirds, bees, and all of God's creation?

The Rev. Marek P. Zabriskie
Rector of Christ Church and the Founder of The Bible Challenge
Greenwich, Connecticut

Questions

What animal or animals most intrigue you? What flora and fauna most captivate you? What are you doing to help preserve them?

Have you taken time to learn more about one of God's creatures or creations and study it? With Google, all things are possible. Consider studying one creature, plant, or tree and going deeper in your knowledge of it so that you can become more aware, more appreciative, and more inspired to be good stewards of God's creation.

Prayer

God above us, God below us, God all around us, God within us, be now the God that builds a bridge for your truth to flow from your divine being into our hearts and minds. Enable us to make changes in our lives to lead a simpler, less materialistic life and help us become more deeply aware of the wonders around us so that we can be faithful caretakers of your creation. *Amen.*

Amos 4:7-13

⁷And I also withheld the rain from you when there were still three months to the harvest; I would send rain on one city, and send no rain on another city; one field would be rained upon, and the field on which it did not rain withered; ⁸so two or three towns wandered to one town to drink water, and were not satisfied; yet you did not return to me, says the LORD.

⁹I struck you with blight and mildew; I laid waste your gardens and your vineyards; the locust devoured your fig trees and your olive trees; yet you did not return to me, says the LORD.

¹⁰I sent among you a pestilence after the manner of Egypt; I killed your young men with the sword; I carried away your horses; and I made the stench of your camp go up into your nostrils; yet you did not return to me, says the LORD. ¹¹I overthrew some of you, as when God overthrew Sodom and Gomorrah, and you were like a brand snatched from the fire; yet you did not return to me, says the LORD.

¹²Therefore thus I will do to you, O Israel; because I will do this to you, prepare to meet your God, O Israel! ¹³For lo, the one who forms the mountains, creates the wind, reveals his thoughts to mortals, makes the morning darkness, and treads on the heights of the earth—the LORD, the God of hosts, is his name!

Reflection

There is a rawness, a lack of safety in living closely in community—whether that is human community or within the rhythms of the more-than-human community. Viewing a mountain from a car makes it easy to feel awe; being trapped on a mountain during a storm is an entirely different experience. Amos knew both the rawness of farming (he self identifies as a shepherd and a dresser of fig trees) and of community living (as he rails against the corruption of Israel).

This passage from Amos is violent, vengeful, and challenging to read. God promises to rain down destruction on the people. As we begin to see the impacts of industrialized capitalism on our planet, perhaps this passage makes more sense. Rather than a causal relationship of "we act, and God punishes," perhaps Amos is revealing a descriptive account.

In our modern world, it might read something like this: If we turn from God by ravenously burning fossil fuels, then the temperatures will rise, and the oceans will boil. If we turn from God and level mountains for metals or coal, then the rivers will turn to toxic mud, and our children will die. If we deforest the world with continual expansion, then our climates will collapse, and we will experience raging wildfires, drought, and flood. But God offers us another way, and the remedy is relationship. "Prepare to meet your God." God offers to meet us face to face—to draw us back in and face us when we cannot seem to face her.

The Rev. Rachel Field
Episcopal Priest and Farmer
Randolph, Vermont

Questions

Sit with this text in your body. Where do you feel tension or soreness when you imagine this break of relationship with God played out through the world? Where do you feel lightness when you imagine God reaching out to us?

Have you ever been in a situation where you have experienced God in nature but as raw power rather than majestic or beautiful? How did or does that impact your relationship with God?

When you read passages like this one that are potentially disturbing, how do you talk to God about them? What do you learn about yourself when you do talk to God about passages like this?

Prayer

Mountain Shaper, you hold all things and exceed all things: turn us with your presence from paths of destruction and settle us once more against the curve of your breast that we may be enfolded ever more deeply in your eternal reconciling love, through the power of your beloved Son who levels the mountains and lifts the valleys. *Amen.*

Matthew 7:12-28

¹²"In everything do to others as you would have them do to you; for this is the law and the prophets. ¹³"Enter through the narrow gate; for the gate is wide and the road is easy that leads to destruction, and there are many who take it. ¹⁴For the gate is narrow and the road is hard that leads to life, and there are few who find it.

¹⁵"Beware of false prophets, who come to you in sheep's clothing but inwardly are ravenous wolves. ¹⁶You will know them by their fruits. Are grapes gathered from thorns, or figs from thistles? ¹⁷In the same way, every good tree bears good fruit, but the bad tree bears bad fruit. ¹⁸A good tree cannot bear bad fruit, nor can a bad tree bear good fruit. ¹⁹Every tree that does not bear good fruit is cut down and thrown into the fire. Thus you will know them by their fruits.

²¹"Not everyone who says to me, 'Lord, Lord,' will enter the kingdom of heaven, but only the one who does the will of my Father in heaven. ²²On that day many will say to me, 'Lord, Lord, did we not prophesy in your name, and cast out demons in your name, and do many deeds of power in your name?' ²³Then I will declare to them, 'I never knew you; go away from me, you evildoers.' ²⁴"Everyone then who hears these words of mine and acts on them will be like a wise man who built his house on rock. ²⁵The rain fell, the floods came, and the winds blew and beat on that house, but it did not fall, because it had been founded on rock. ²⁶And everyone who hears these words of mine and does not act on them will be like a foolish man who built his house on sand. ²⁷The rain fell, and the

floods came, and the winds blew and beat against that house, and it fell—and great was its fall!"

²⁸Now when Jesus had finished saying these things, the crowds were astounded at his teaching.

Reflection

Jesus's embrace of what we call the "Golden Rule" is unreserved. Here, as well as in numerous other passages, he offers these words as a universal moral guide for all our actions: "In everything do to others as you would have them do to you."

Jesus is not alone. The premise of the Golden Rule can be found at the core of every major world religion. And why is that? Adherence to the Golden Rule requires both transparency and sincerity in our interactions; it banishes hypocrisy. One thing more: as the rest of this passage makes clear, we live out the Golden Rule through our faithful actions. In the Gospel of Luke, Jesus again makes this point: we are to love our neighbors as ourselves (Luke 10:27). When the lawyer asks, "Who is my neighbor?" Jesus shares the story of the Good Samaritan, one of the most well-known illustrations of the Golden Rule.

The Golden Rule has served humanity well for centuries. Every congregation I know has numerous initiatives to reach out to and support neighbors in need across town—and across the globe. But there is a new reality that people of faith must now take into account. If we continue our normal behavior over the coming years, we will sentence our children, grandchildren, and future generations to live on an uninhabitable planet.

Thank God for climate scientists who have been sounding the alarm for decades. Thank God for engineers who have provided many solutions humanity needs to make a just transition to a sustainable, renewable energy system.

And what of us? As people of faith, God is calling us to embrace a new moral compass. We can call it Golden Rule 2.0. Let us expand our understanding of neighbor by recognizing that all creatures alive today and those yet to be born are our neighbors. Let us acknowledge the grave impact our generation has on the conditions that would allow future generations to thrive, perhaps even survive. Let us reorient our hearts, lives, and laws to honor and respect the interdependence of all creation.

The Rev. Dr. Jim Antal
Special Advisor on Climate Justice to
United Church of Christ General Minister and President
Norwich, Vermont

Questions

How does the practice of the Golden Rule require transparency and sincerity? How does it banish hypocrisy?

What actions could you and your family take to live out Golden Rule 2.0?

What actions could our legal, corporate, and governmental systems take to live out Golden Rule 2.0, and how could you and your congregation advocate for such actions?

Prayer

O God of mercy and justice, disturb our longing for business as usual and fill our hearts with gratitude for the opportunity to witness amidst this crisis as we enact the truths that will free all of your creation from our captivity to fossil fuels. Grant us the quiet joy that emerges in unexpected moments as we align our lives with your call, seeking climate justice and the redemption of your creation. *Amen.*

Matthew 13:1-23

¹That same day Jesus went out of the house and sat beside the sea. ²Such great crowds gathered around him that he got into a boat and sat there, while the whole crowd stood on the beach. ³And he told them many things in parables, saying: "Listen! A sower went out to sow. ⁴And as he sowed, some seeds fell on the path, and the birds came and ate them up. ⁵Other seeds fell on rocky ground, where they did not have much soil, and they sprang up quickly, since they had no depth of soil. ⁶But when the sun rose, they were scorched; and since they had no root, they withered away. ⁷Other seeds fell among thorns, and the thorns grew up and choked them. ⁸Other seeds fell on good soil and brought forth grain, some a hundredfold, some sixty, some thirty. ⁹Let anyone with ears listen!"

¹⁰Then the disciples came and asked him, "Why do you speak to them in parables?" ¹¹He answered, "To you it has been given to know the secrets of the kingdom of heaven, but to them it has not been given. ¹²For to those who have, more will be given, and they will have an abundance; but from those who have nothing, even what they have will be taken away. ¹³The reason I speak to them in parables is that 'seeing they do not perceive, and hearing they do not listen, nor do they understand.' ¹⁴With them indeed is fulfilled the prophecy of Isaiah that says: 'You will indeed listen, but never understand, and you will indeed look, but never perceive. ¹⁵For this people's heart has grown dull, and their ears are hard of hearing, and they have shut their eyes; so that they might not look with their eyes,

and listen with their ears, and understand with their heart and turn—and I would heal them.' ¹⁶But blessed are your eyes, for they see, and your ears, for they hear. ¹⁷Truly I tell you, many prophets and righteous people longed to see what you see, but did not see it, and to hear what you hear, but did not hear it. ¹⁸"Hear then the parable of the sower. ¹⁹When anyone hears the word of the kingdom and does not understand it, the evil one comes and snatches away what is sown in the heart; this is what was sown on the path. ²⁰As for what was sown on rocky ground, this is the one who hears the word and immediately receives it with joy; ²¹yet such a person has no root, but endures only for a while, and when trouble or persecution arises on account of the word, that person immediately falls away. ²²As for what was sown among thorns, this is the one who hears the word, but the cares of the world and the lure of wealth choke the word, and it yields nothing. ²³But as for what was sown on good soil, this is the one who hears the word and understands it, who indeed bears fruit and yields, in one case a hundredfold, in another sixty, and in another thirty."

The Creation Care Bible Challenge

Reflection

"We are dirt and to dirt we shall return" is a mantra of faith.

That is the humbling and freeing truth of the human condition. It makes sense that Jesus was all about dirt. He wrote notes in the dirt in the face of danger, used dirt to make a healing mud, and told the disciples to shake it off their feet when they found no peace in a town.

In the heart of Matthew's Gospel, Jesus is in the thick of dirt. He is giving the disciples a road map of how to travel into cities, preaching and teaching. He is focused on dirt and seeds and what needs to be rooted and tilled and tended in the midst of foreign occupation, poverty, and hostility. He is inviting us to grow good fruit and to weep at the parched nature of our being. We need to till the earth of our hearts, watering it and weeding the unruly places that cause us to stumble.

Dirt is universal and timeless, thank God. Dirt is the community in which all things grow. One person does not get good seed and good soil and another just rocky ground or a path. It's all part of the same ground, and, in community, a field of rocky dirt can become rich soil. Soil is connected. There are times to remove the rocks and add nutrients. Rocky soil becomes aerated by digging up roots and rocks and using compost to make it rich. Dry soil becomes fertile with water, and thin soil, easily scorched, becomes thick by building up beds, digging ditches for irrigation, and allowing seasons to lie fallow.

Dirt will be our companion our whole lives; together we can make a rich field that will bear unbelievably sweet fruit.

The Rev. Becca Stevens
Author and Founder of Magdalene House
Nashville, Tennessee

Questions

How does it help us in creation care work to see ourselves as dirt?

Where do you see the rocky soil in you?

Where is the rich soil in your life that you are allowing to grow a great harvest?

Prayer

God, in the dusty clay you formed me. I am the soil that needs to be tilled, planted, and watered to grow new seed. It is not easy for me to dig out the rocks, take seasons to lie fallow, and to work in community to make the harvest rich. Give me the grace and peace to grow and love this world and all its dirt. *Amen.*

Matthew 13:24-29

[24]He put before them another parable: "The kingdom of heaven may be compared to someone who sowed good seed in his field; [25]but while everybody was asleep, an enemy came and sowed weeds among the wheat, and then went away. [26]So when the plants came up and bore grain, then the weeds appeared as well. [27]And the slaves of the householder came and said to him, 'Master, did you not sow good seed in your field? Where, then, did these weeds come from?' [28]He answered, 'An enemy has done this.' The slaves said to him, 'Then do you want us to go and gather them?' [29]But he replied, 'No; for in gathering the weeds you would uproot the wheat along with them.'"

Reflection

A recent report from the Intergovernmental Panel on Climate Change (IPCC), the UN body for assessing the science related to climate change, shows significant climate change. Based on research and review of studies from around the world, it offers unequivocal evidence of the extent to which we have failed to taken care of the global vineyards, wheat fields, farms, agricultural pastures, forests, rice paddies, taro patches, and gardens entrusted into our care by the greatest and most trustworthy sower of all.

To really understand this parable from Matthew's Gospel, it is helpful to understand that Jesus is describing the kingdom of God. Jesus is sowing "gospel" seeds throughout the world by way of raising up faithful Christians. But at the same time, the enemy is in the world spreading harmful or destructive seeds.

This parable turns on its head when you consider that those responsible for the contemporary harm and destruction of God's created world are not just "the enemy" or those who are evil but also many of those of us who lay claim to being the Body of Christ, to being the body of the faithful. We are failing as faith-filled stewards and guardians of God's infinitely perfect created planet Earth.

It is way too convenient for us to simply lay the blame at the feet of the "enemy who has done this." As the IPCC report shows, the massive and ongoing failure of all in the human community to care for God's creation is causing irreversible and utterly devastating harm to our planet, our ecology, our Mother the Earth.

It isn't always simple, and neither should it be, to discern the differences between those who belong to the kingdom and those who do not. It is all too easy for Christians to laud it over non-Christians. Toward the end of this parable, it becomes more apparent that Jesus calls and blesses us to be the "good seeds," acting with selflessness and courageous discipleship. It is not for us to discern the "weeds" in our midst—that task is for One much higher than anyone of us.

Dr. Jenny Te Paa Daniel (Te Rarawa)
Te Mareikura (the Esteemed Indigenous Professor) at the
National Centre for Peace and Conflict Studies,
Otago University, Dunedin
Aitutaki, Cook Islands, and Auckland, New Zealand

Questions

What is your church family doing to raise climate change issues and take concrete steps to address its devastating effects?

Do you invite experts in climate change to help you understand the extent to which global warming is causing catastrophic damage, especially to low-lying islands and communities around the world?

Prayer

God of justice, God of all living things, instill in us a heart for climate justice and a heart for ensuring that Mother Earth, as part of your most precious creation, is accorded the protection and care you always expected of us. *Amen.*

Matthew 13:31-32

[31]He put before them another parable: "The kingdom of heaven is like a mustard seed that someone took and sowed in his field; [32]it is the smallest of all the seeds, but when it has grown it is the greatest of shrubs and becomes a tree, so that the birds of the air come and make nests in its branches."

Reflection

South Africa is one of the most biologically diverse countries in the world. Our Cape Floristic Kingdom, at the southwestern tip of Africa, boasts more than 9,000 indigenous plant species, the vast majority occurring nowhere else on earth. Designated as a UNESCO World Heritage Site, the area covers less than half a percent of the land mass of the continent but holds one in five of its plants. These plants are essential for the local economy and tourism as well as for producing edible, medicinal, and ornamental plants.

Since 1900, dozens of plants from this area have become extinct. One strategy to slow down further loss is the conservation of indigenous seeds. Seeds hold all the information about a plant, and some of the plants previously thought to be extinct have been regrown from stored seeds. Many areas previously damaged by fire or human activity have been restored by sowing the seeds of plants known to have grown there.

In Matthew 13:31-32, Jesus compares the kingdom of heaven to a seed. Jesus teaches that the mustard seed is small compared to most other seeds, but the resultant plant is big compared to other plants. The leaves of the mustard plant can be used for food, and the seeds can be ground for spices or oil. From a small seed, many can benefit.

We might look at the parable of the mustard seed as a metaphor for how the Holy Spirit grows in each of us—it starts out small. Yet, as we nurture our faith in God, the Holy Spirit infuses every part of our being, eventually becoming more influential in our lives than our ego, our past, and even our fears. The seed planted in you has all the information needed to achieve God's purpose in and through you.

The Creation Care Bible Challenge

May God the Holy Spirit so grow in you, healing the damaged areas in your life and the world and restoring God's beauty witnessed by all.

The Rev. Shaun Cozett
Rector of St. Paul's Bree Street, South Africa
Cape Town, South Africa

Questions

Are you able to sit still and allow the Holy Spirit to minister to you? Do you listen to the guiding of the small voice deep inside?

What is God asking you to do to restore that which has been damaged?

Prayer

Holy Spirit of our God, thank you for living in me and guiding my life. Help me to see brokenness and pain, not with eyes of despair but with eyes of faith. Fill me with your love and power that I may know your will; and use me to restore your creation, both in me and around me. *Amen.*

Matthew 17:1-8

¹Six days later, Jesus took with him Peter and James and his brother John and led them up a high mountain, by themselves. ²And he was transfigured before them, and his face shone like the sun, and his clothes became dazzling white. ³Suddenly there appeared to them Moses and Elijah, talking with him. ⁴Then Peter said to Jesus, "Lord, it is good for us to be here; if you wish, I will make three dwellings here, one for you, one for Moses, and one for Elijah." ⁵While he was still speaking, suddenly a bright cloud overshadowed them, and from the cloud a voice said, "This is my Son, the Beloved; with him I am well pleased; listen to him!" ⁶When the disciples heard this, they fell to the ground and were overcome by fear. ⁷But Jesus came and touched them, saying, "Get up and do not be afraid." ⁸And when they looked up, they saw no one except Jesus himself alone.

Reflection

Mountain peaks are ever majestic. Big or small, they command their surroundings and offer hikers and pilgrims a glimpse of natural beauty and connection bordering on the transcendent.

Humanity has long sought the Holy One on rocky summits. In such a place, Moses received the Ten Commandments, and Elijah learned his mission. Jesus does the same. Journeying atop the mountain with his followers Peter, James, and John, Jesus encounters God's being so powerfully that his humanity is transfigured into divinity.

The mystical presence of Moses and Elijah testify that Jesus fulfills the law and the prophets. The cloud of the Spirit and the voice of the Father proclaim Jesus's divine Son-ship. The message is bewilderingly clear: Jesus is God the Son incarnate, the Messiah, the Christ. On the mountain, Jesus's identity and destiny are revealed, and so is that of all those who follow him, for to behold him is to become ever more like him.

This passage stands at the heart of eastern Christian spirituality, and when we consider the world in which we live and all we have done and left undone in our lives, it is not difficult to understand why. Who among us does not long to hear our Father's words: "This is my daughter, this is my son, whom I love"? In the face of widespread environmental degradation, intractable armed conflicts, and haunting histories, the peace of eternal union with God is ecstasy indeed.

The Rev. Canon Nicholas T. Porter
Founding Director, Jerusalem Peacebuilders
New England, Texas, and the Holy Lands

Questions

What is the difference between *transformation* and *transfiguration*? How does this difference reveal our Lord's grace in your life?

How do Jesus and the prophets envision the whole world being transfigured? What will that transfiguration look like?

Prayer

Almighty God, who on a mountain revealed your well-beloved Son, open our eyes to your life-giving presence in the world around us. Strengthen our minds and bodies to heal and serve all creation, and mercifully grant that when our days end, we shall awake in Jesus's likeness. All this we pray in the Name of your transfigured Son. *Amen.*

Matthew 21:18-22

[18]In the morning, when he returned to the city, he was hungry. [19]And seeing a fig tree by the side of the road, he went to it and found nothing at all on it but leaves. Then he said to it, "May no fruit ever come from you again!" And the fig tree withered at once. [20]When the disciples saw it, they were amazed, saying, "How did the fig tree wither at once?" [21]Jesus answered them, "Truly I tell you, if you have faith and do not doubt, not only will you do what has been done to the fig tree, but even if you say to this mountain, 'Be lifted up and thrown into the sea,' it will be done. [22]Whatever you ask for in prayer with faith, you will receive."

Reflection

I've been teaching biblical creation care for two decades. I don't think there is a passage that I get more questions about than this one. To many, it seems so out of character for Jesus. In fact, this is the only incident the Bible records of Jesus harming anything. Does God have something against trees?

If we lift our gaze from this withered specimen and cast our eyes across the vast landscape of the Bible, we get a different story. We see trees playing a pivotal role in scripture, from Genesis to Revelation. There is a tree planted on the first page of the Bible. The first psalm tells us to be like a tree. On the first page of the New Testament, God shares Jesus's family tree, and the last chapter of the Bible all takes place in the shade of the tree at the center of heaven, the leaves of which are for the "healing of the nations."

Major theological events in the Bible often have a tree marking the spot, and major characters in scripture have associated trees. In Genesis, God awards Joseph with a high compliment: Joseph *is* a tree; "his branches run over the wall" (Genesis 49:22).

So why does Jesus kill a tree? First, because it's a *fig* tree. Although Jesus was surrounded by palms, cedars, and oaks, the only genus of tree ever mentioned by Jesus is the Ficus. When Nathanael marvels that Jesus knows him, Christ reminds Nathanael that he saw him under a fig tree. We humans have a long history of trying to hide from God behind fig trees. Jesus's encounter with the fig tree reminds us that once Christ steps onto the earth, there can be no more hiding from God.

Secondly, Jesus is illustrating what happens when we do not yield fruit. All of creation was made by and for Christ. Jesus hungered, and the fig tree failed to feed him. The fig tree, like each of us, withers and dies when we fail to bear fruit for the Kingdom of God.

Matthew Sleeth, MD
Cofounder of Blessed Earth
Lexington, Kentucky

Question

What is the fruit of your life?

Do you feel like a barren or a fruitful tree? What are some of the fruitful gifts you share with others?

Does a branch of your life (or a sin) need to be pruned to make your life more fruitful?

Prayer

Heavenly Father, no tree seeks darkness. All of creation obeys you. Grant that we might grow toward you as oaks of righteousness. Separate us from all sin that keeps us from bearing fruit. Through your death on a tree, allow us to eat from the Tree of Life with you in paradise. *Amen.*

Luke 12:22-34

²²He said to his disciples, "Therefore I tell you, do not worry about your life, what you will eat, or about your body, what you will wear. ²³For life is more than food, and the body more than clothing. ²⁴Consider the ravens: they neither sow nor reap, they have neither storehouse nor barn, and yet God feeds them. Of how much more value are you than the birds! ²⁵And can any of you by worrying add a single hour to your span of life? ²⁶If then you are not able to do so small a thing as that, why do you worry about the rest? ²⁷Consider the lilies, how they grow: they neither toil nor spin; yet I tell you, even Solomon in all his glory was not clothed like one of these. ²⁸But if God so clothes the grass of the field, which is alive today and tomorrow is thrown into the oven, how much more will he clothe you—you of little faith! ²⁹And do not keep striving for what you are to eat and what you are to drink, and do not keep worrying. ³⁰For it is the nations of the world that strive after all these things, and your Father knows that you need them. ³¹Instead, strive for his kingdom, and these things will be given to you as well. ³²"Do not be afraid, little flock, for it is your Father's good pleasure to give you the kingdom. ³³Sell your possessions, and give alms. Make purses for yourselves that do not wear out, an unfailing treasure in heaven, where no thief comes near and no moth destroys. ³⁴For where your treasure is, there your heart will be also."

Reflection

Jesus's insistence on not worrying about seemingly unimportant matters is a lesson in what it means to be a people of faith. We naturally worry about matters of concern in our lives, community, and world. The COVID-19 pandemic caused the whole world to worry together. We feared the unknown impact of the pandemic on the whole of humanity. We faced the real threat of mass death on a scale we have never seen in recent times. We saw institutions that were supposed to help prevent death rendered helpless. We had good reason to worry, to be concerned, to fear. That anxiety has not subsided.

Jesus wants us to put these concerns in perspective. Of course, we want to know what we will have to eat, where we can find drink, what we will cover our bodies with, and where we will rest our heads at night. This is especially true if we have families and children to feed, clothe, and house. They depend on us to provide for their security, welfare, and well-being. This worrying intensifies when we face threats such as hunger, poverty, homelessness, disease, unemployment, depression, violence, drought, and flooding.

Only through the eyes of faith can we turn to God to address our worries, to have our prayers heard and answered. Consider the birds, Jesus says. You have more value than birds and flowers, yet they do not worry about anything. God's extravagant love casts out fear. The hope that Jesus gives us overcomes despair. Kingdom faith conquers anxiety and worry. By having faith in Jesus, we have moved from possessing little faith to gaining the greatest hope in the world.

The Rt. Rev. Te Kitohi Pikaahu
Anglican Bishop of Tai Tokerau
Northland-Auckland, New Zealand

Questions

In the face of all adversity, is our faith strong enough to put our total trust in the God of hope? Can we see beyond our own trials and tribulations to seek God's will and purpose for our lives, communities, and world?

Do we have the capacity to reach out in faith, to move forward in hope, to receive the blessing of God's love, God's grace, and God's peace?

Prayer

God of hope and goodness, we give you thanks and praise for the world and for your presence in and throughout the whole of creation. We praise you that whatever worry we may face in our lives, in our communities, and in our world, we need only seek your kingdom and your righteousness, and in doing so, look to you to cast out all fear and overcome anxiety and despair. We praise you for the treasures we have stored in heaven, which is the fulfillment of the promises of blessing, grace, and peace in your kingdom. We make this prayer in the Name of Jesus Christ, your Son, our Savior, and Redeemer. *Amen.*

The Creation Care Bible Challenge

John 3:11-21

[11]Very truly, I tell you, we speak of what we know and testify to what we have seen; yet you do not receive our testimony. [12]If I have told you about earthly things and you do not believe, how can you believe if I tell you about heavenly things? [13]No one has ascended into heaven except the one who descended from heaven, the Son of Man. [14]And just as Moses lifted up the serpent in the wilderness, so must the Son of Man be lifted up, [15]that whoever believes in him may have eternal life. [16]For God so loved the world that he gave his only Son, so that everyone who believes in him may not perish but may have eternal life. [17]Indeed, God did not send the Son into the world to condemn the world, but in order that the world might be saved through him. [18]Those who believe in him are not condemned; but those who do not believe are condemned already, because they have not believed in the name of the only Son of God. [19]And this is the judgment, that the light has come into the world, and people loved darkness rather than light because their deeds were evil. [20]For all who do evil hate the light and do not come to the light, so that their deeds may not be exposed. [21]But those who do what is true come to the light, so that it may be clearly seen that their deeds have been done in God.

Reflection

There may be no passage of scripture more familiar than John 3:16: "For God so loved the world that he gave his only Son." It's on bumper stickers, roadside signs, T-shirts. If you know nothing else about Christianity, you may very well know this passage.

We commonly emphasize the implications for human salvation—that God came among us in Jesus and was brutally slain by the authorities as part of a divine effort to reconcile alienated humanity with God and one another. But it is past time to expand our scope and proclaim a deeper truth.

God so loved *the world*. And not only in the past tense: God continues to love and will always love what God has created. That includes us humans, but we are by no means the only recipients of God's love. We know this because scripture tells us the breadth of God's embrace and affection. God's love envelops the great skies and zeroes in on the tiny sparrow. God chooses to be felt in the sacred ground on which we dwell and heard in the fish of the sea. Everywhere we gaze, every part of the natural world, not only do we witness something God provided for our flourishing, but also we see that which God loves and created for its own sake.

God's love for this world is strong, fierce and self-giving. "Indeed, God did not send the Son into the world to condemn the world, but in order that the world might be saved through him" (John 3:17). If this divine circle of love and salvation encompasses the whole of creation, that changes my life. As a follower of Jesus, I've been baptized and reborn to see the world through his eyes, to love what he loves, to protect what he protects. As his disciple, I hear the call to sacrifice my comfort and convenience, conserve resources, lighten my carbon footprint, and advocate for change on behalf of the creation he loves so much he gave his life.

The Rev. Canon Stephanie Spellers
Canon to the Presiding Bishop for
Evangelism, Reconciliation, and Creation Care
New York City, New York

Questions

Where in the natural world do you see signs of God's love?

If God loves the world, and we love God and love what God loves, how does that change how you live in the world? What might you choose to do? What might you choose not to do?

Prayer

O God, your love extends higher and broader than my human imagination can grasp. Expand the compassion of my small heart, that I might fall in love with the skies, lands, and fellow creatures with whom I share this planet, all of whom are so dear to you. In the Name of Jesus, whose will is the salvation of all living things. *Amen.*

John 4:13-14

[13]Jesus said to her, "Everyone who drinks of this water will be thirsty again, [14]but those who drink of the water that I will give them will never be thirsty. The water that I will give will become in them a spring of water gushing up to eternal life."

Reflection

The drama of Jesus's encounter with the woman at the well has inspired the classic Gospel song, "Jesus Gave Me Water" (find the version by the Soul Stirrers with a young Sam Cooke). Its refrain is: "Jesus gave me water, and it was not from the well."

What is this living water? What is this thirst that H^2O cannot quench? Psalm 42:1 reads,

"As a deer longs for flowing streams, so my soul longs for you, O God." In the same way that every biological creature seeks water, humans long for, in addition, something more. The psalmist uses the word "God" for this something more, but we could also term it as meaning, ultimacy, *raison d'être*.

Humans are meaning-makers, pattern-tracers, and storytellers. This capacity gives humans a special role in the care for creation. If we imagine our planet as a single body in which the rainforests are lungs and the water cycle the bloodstream, then humans are the brain. As the physicist Marcelo Gleiser put it, "We humans . . . are how the universe thinks."

This capacity for reflection makes our species no more special but also no less essential. As the thinking organ of the world's body, we are called to be conscious of the health of all life.

The Rev. Dr. Gregory Mobley
Professor of Hebrew Bible at Yale Divinity School
New Haven, Connecticut

Questions

How can we humans play our part, alongside other flora and fauna, in *shalom*, divine harmony?

As you move through the world, always ask yourself, "How do the animate and inanimate aspects of our fellow creatures contribute to the body of the world?"

Prayer

O Lord, how manifold are your works! In Wisdom you created them all. Through your breath that hovered on the face of the waters, all life has been baptized into a single body and made to drink of a single Spirit. We praise the One who so arranged the body. If one member suffers, all suffer together with it; if one member is honored, all rejoice together with it. *Amen.*

John 17:1-26

¹After Jesus had spoken these words, he looked up to heaven and said, "Father, the hour has come; glorify your Son so that the Son may glorify you, ²since you have given him authority over all people, to give eternal life to all whom you have given him. ³And this is eternal life, that they may know you, the only true God, and Jesus Christ whom you have sent. ⁴I glorified you on earth by finishing the work that you gave me to do. ⁵So now, Father, glorify me in your own presence with the glory that I had in your presence before the world existed.

⁶"I have made your name known to those whom you gave me from the world. They were yours, and you gave them to me, and they have kept your word. ⁷Now they know that everything you have given me is from you; ⁸for the words that you gave to me I have given to them, and they have received them and know in truth that I came from you; and they have believed that you sent me. ⁹I am asking on their behalf; I am not asking on behalf of the world, but on behalf of those whom you gave me, because they are yours. ¹⁰All mine are yours, and yours are mine; and I have been glorified in them.

¹¹And now I am no longer in the world, but they are in the world, and I am coming to you. Holy Father, protect them in your name that you have given me, so that they may be one, as we are one. ¹²While I was with them, I protected them in your name that you have given me. I guarded them, and not one of them was lost except the one destined to be lost, so that the scripture might be fulfilled. ¹³But now I am

coming to you, and I speak these things in the world so that they may have my joy made complete in themselves. ¹⁴I have given them your word, and the world has hated them because they do not belong to the world, just as I do not belong to the world. ¹⁵I am not asking you to take them out of the world, but I ask you to protect them from the evil one. ¹⁶They do not belong to the world, just as I do not belong to the world.

¹⁷Sanctify them in the truth; your word is truth. ¹⁸As you have sent me into the world, so I have sent them into the world. ¹⁹And for their sakes I sanctify myself, so that they also may be sanctified in truth.

²⁰"I ask not only on behalf of these, but also on behalf of those who will believe in me through their word, ²¹that they may all be one. As you, Father, are in me and I am in you, may they also be in us, so that the world may believe that you have sent me. ²²The glory that you have given me I have given them, so that they may be one, as we are one, ²³I in them and you in me, that they may become completely one, so that the world may know that you have sent me and have loved them even as you have loved me.

²⁴"Father, I desire that those also, whom you have given me, may be with me where I am, to see my glory, which you have given me because you loved me before the foundation of the world. ²⁵"Righteous Father, the world does not know you, but I know you; and these know that you have sent me. ²⁶I made your name known to them, and I will make it known, so that the love with which you have loved me may be in them, and I in them."

Reflection

Jesus announces to his disciples that "the moment is at hand;" he has fulfilled God's purpose to be an example of God's power and glory on earth. Now then, how will the disciples make sense of Jesus's life? How will God's glory be conveyed after Jesus is gone? Perhaps Jesus is saying, "Look, friends, you won't have me around to teach and make sense of what God's power means to you and all humanity. So, pay attention! The glory of God's power to sustain creation is passed on, as it was to me, and will now be available to you simply by believing that God is the only God to provide eternal life. That is the word from the only One."

I received the "word" from my parents, who incorporated me into the church and subsequent baptism; my faith throughout church life took the forms of service: choirboy, acolyte, vestryman, Diocesan Council, national conventions.

Living this faith in my work as an entrepreneur was challenging in a culture of materialism. For instance, I asked my board of directors at Tom's of Maine to create a statement of beliefs to go alongside our mission statement. "We believe that people and nature have inherent worth and deserve our respect," we stated. To operate the business with this belief, we created radical policies. These include a stewardship model for guiding product development, sharing of 10 percent of profits for nonprofits, giving 5 percent volunteering from paid time for the community, providing flexible hours to accommodate personal family demands, and parental leave at times of birth. And this was all in the 1980s. We became a powerful example to hundreds of companies later who came to believe that a business can be financially successful while behaving responsibly with creation.

Committing my life's journey to the only God gives me courage to do the things God has in mind for me. For me, it is confidence in the word given to me by my parents, church community, and others who believe. That has given me freedom to be who I am.

Tom Chappell
Co-Founder of Tom's of Maine and the Ramblers Way Farm
Kennebunk, Maine

Questions

When your intuition calls you to care for creation, do you need board approval or God's support?

Does your risk call for edging out gradually toward your goal or is it a complete leap of faith?

Prayer

My time is at hand. Carry me, Lord, to the other side of the river for I see no bridge. I must reach the other side. I give myself to thee in faith that my work may please thee; use me as you will. I am thy servant. Thank you, God. *Amen.*

John 21:1-14

¹After these things Jesus showed himself again to the disciples by the Sea of Tiberias; and he showed himself in this way. ²Gathered there together were Simon Peter, Thomas called the Twin, Nathanael of Cana in Galilee, the sons of Zebedee, and two others of his disciples. ³Simon Peter said to them, "I am going fishing." They said to him, "We will go with you." They went out and got into the boat, but that night they caught nothing. ⁴Just after daybreak, Jesus stood on the beach; but the disciples did not know that it was Jesus. ⁵Jesus said to them, "Children, you have no fish, have you?" They answered him, "No." ⁶He said to them, "Cast the net to the right side of the boat, and you will find some." So they cast it, and now they were not able to haul it in because there were so many fish. ⁷That disciple whom Jesus loved said to Peter, "It is the Lord!" When Simon Peter heard that it was the Lord, he put on some clothes, for he was naked, and jumped into the sea. ⁸But the other disciples came in the boat, dragging the net full of fish, for they were not far from the land, only about a hundred yards off. ⁹When they had gone ashore, they saw a charcoal fire there, with fish on it, and bread. ¹⁰Jesus said to them, "Bring some of the fish that you have just caught." ¹¹So Simon Peter went aboard and hauled the net ashore, full of large fish, a hundred fifty-three of them; and though there were so many, the net was not torn. ¹²Jesus said to them, "Come and have breakfast." Now none of the disciples dared to ask him, "Who are you?" because they knew it was the Lord. ¹³Jesus came and

took the bread and gave it to them, and did the same with the fish. [14]This was now the third time that Jesus appeared to the disciples after he was raised from the dead.

Reflection

One night years ago, fishing off the beach in Rhode Island, a friend asked me why I thought that Jesus chose fishermen to be his apostles. I didn't really have an answer. He told me that Jesus could have approached anyone and performed his miracles for them, but he chose fishermen because they were acute observers of their environment. Jesus also needed to be sure that when he performed a miracle, the people seeing it would recognize, without a doubt and without any possible exception, that it was indeed a miracle.

If you perform a miracle to a person on the streets of a city, they may laugh at you and suspect that you are a trickster or a joker. If you are going to convince people to follow you because you are God in human form, my friend told me, then you had better choose people who, upon seeing something incongruous to what they know, will have no other choice but to believe with every quiver of their nervous system that what they witnessed was indeed a true miracle.

And so, Jesus came down to the waters of the Sea of Galilee. He came as a total stranger to a bunch of grizzled fishermen, worn by the weather. They acknowledged him. Every day, these fishermen saw the sun come up and go down. They knew the patterns of the weather. They could read the patterns of the waves. The waves and wind had carved them, shaped their bodies. And this total stranger gives them advice: Cast your nets on the other side of the boat. Really, they must have thought. Seriously, is this your fishing advice? Walk to the other side of the boat and cast your nets there?

Why did they listen? We may never know. But they did listen. And when they did what Jesus said, they filled their boat with fish. And that was that. The anonymous man, in one stroke, elevated himself from total stranger to God.

James Prosek
Artist, writer, and naturalist
Easton, Connecticut

Questions

Do you think you'd recognize a miracle if you saw one?

Do you think that if we all had a relationship as intimate with nature as the apostles that we would be better stewards of the environment?

Prayer

Dear God, please inspire us to be better stewards of our natural world. I stand in awe at your creation and the creations of evolution and have been moved by that awe to help protect the diversity of this planet. But we can all do more, and I hope that we will do more before we lose the sources of our awe and inspiration, for we would live a pale existence without them. *Amen.*

Day 44

Acts 14:8-20

8In Lystra there was a man sitting who could not use his feet and had never walked, for he had been crippled from birth. 9He listened to Paul as he was speaking. And Paul, looking at him intently and seeing that he had faith to be healed, 10said in a loud voice, "Stand upright on your feet." And the man sprang up and began to walk. 11When the crowds saw what Paul had done, they shouted in the Lycaonian language, "The gods have come down to us in human form!" 12Barnabas they called Zeus, and Paul they called Hermes, because he was the chief speaker. 13The priest of Zeus, whose temple was just outside the city, brought oxen and garlands to the gates; he and the crowds wanted to offer sacrifice. 14When the apostles Barnabas and Paul heard of it, they tore their clothes and rushed out into the crowd, shouting, 15"Friends, why are you doing this? We are mortals just like you, and we bring you good news, that you should turn from these worthless things to the living God, who made the heaven and the earth and the sea and all that is in them. 16In past generations he allowed all the nations to follow their own ways; 17yet he has not left himself without a witness in doing good—giving you rains from heaven and fruitful seasons, and filling you with food and your hearts with joy." 18Even with these words, they scarcely restrained the crowds from offering sacrifice to them.

19But Jews came there from Antioch and Iconium and won over the crowds. Then they stoned Paul and dragged him out of the city, supposing that he was dead. 20But when the disciples surrounded him, he got up and went into the city. The next day he went on with Barnabas to Derbe.

Reflection

I find the "simplify" signs that are sold in catalogs ironic. Do we need worthless items as a reminder to possess fewer things? I have many worthless things that may provide occasional happiness but actually clutter my home and my heart. My desire for things beyond basic needs consumes energy while distracting me from loving God and God's creation. This desire for increased consumer goods contributes to the destruction of Earth as demand for production stretches the world's resources, creating even more pollution of water, land, and air. Worthless things, too, can be the relentless pursuit of wealth, power, and success that may distract from our focus on seeking a just, equitable, and habitable kingdom here on earth. We become seekers of things that take us away from the living God.

In this passage from the Book of Acts, worthless things include precise, exacting rituals that may lead us to worship the ritual rather than God. Paul and Barnabas remind the crowd that in pursuing worthless things, we forget the kindness of God and risk not hearing the Good News. We are so distracted by worthless things that we may miss the awesomeness of the Creator who "made the heavens and the earth and the sea and everything in them."

If we choose to make quiet prayerful time with God in the beauty of nature, we can be drawn into a deeper personal relationship with God and all creation, turning our energies away from worthless things. Developing such a spiritual practice can fill our hearts with joy and lead us to offer gratitude for the blessings of all creation.

The Rev. Stephanie Johnson
Rector of St. Paul's Episcopal Church
Riverside, Connecticut

Questions

What type of "worthless things" demand your attention? How can you free yourself from the focus on these things and instead turn to the abundance and beauty of God's creation?

What actions can you take to limit your consumption of worthless things to help heal the earth?

Prayer

Creator, help us to celebrate the bounty of your beautiful creation fully. Thank you for sharing the earth with us, all creatures and living beings. Thank you too for giving rain from heaven and crops in their season. Lead us away from seeking worthless things that distract us from you and cause us to destroy that which you have so lovingly created. Loving God, keep us mindful that, in your eyes, all earth is equally sacred and never worthless. Guide us to preserve and protect all creation which you so love. *Amen.*

Acts 17:16-34

[16]While Paul was waiting for them in Athens, he was deeply distressed to see that the city was full of idols. [17]So he argued in the synagogue with the Jews and the devout persons, and also in the marketplace every day with those who happened to be there. [18]Also some Epicurean and Stoic philosophers debated with him. Some said, "What does this babbler want to say?" Others said, "He seems to be a proclaimer of foreign divinities." (This was because he was telling the good news about Jesus and the resurrection.) [19]So they took him and brought him to the Areopagus and asked him, "May we know what this new teaching is that you are presenting? [20]It sounds rather strange to us, so we would like to know what it means." [21]Now all the Athenians and the foreigners living there would spend their time in nothing but telling or hearing something new.

[22]Then Paul stood in front of the Areopagus and said, "Athenians, I see how extremely religious you are in every way. [23]For as I went through the city and looked carefully at the objects of your worship, I found among them an altar with the inscription, 'To an unknown god.' What therefore you worship as unknown, this I proclaim to you. [24]The God who made the world and everything in it, he who is Lord of heaven and earth, does not live in shrines made by human hands, [25]nor is he served by human hands, as though he needed anything, since he himself gives to all mortals life and breath and all things. [26]From one ancestor he made all nations to inhabit the whole earth, and he allotted the times of their existence and

the boundaries of the places where they would live, 27so that they would search for God and perhaps grope for him and find him—though indeed he is not far from each one of us. 28For 'In him we live and move and have our being'; as even some of your own poets have said, 'For we too are his offspring.' 29Since we are God's offspring, we ought not to think that the deity is like gold, or silver, or stone, an image formed by the art and imagination of mortals. 30While God has overlooked the times of human ignorance, now he commands all people everywhere to repent, 31because he has fixed a day on which he will have the world judged in righteousness by a man whom he has appointed, and of this he has given assurance to all by raising him from the dead."

32When they heard of the resurrection of the dead, some scoffed; but others said, "We will hear you again about this." 33At that point Paul left them. 34But some of them joined him and became believers, including Dionysius the Areopagite and a woman named Damaris, and others with them.

Reflection

In this passage from the Acts of the Apostle, Paul reminds us that the God who commanded all things to come into being cannot be confined to human-made shrines. This God is both the source and sustainer of all life and breath. As the one who gives life to all things, God needs nothing from humans. We find these truths echoed in Eucharistic Prayer C of the Book of Common Prayer (page 370):

At your command all things came to be: the vast expanse of interstellar space, galaxies, suns, the planets in their courses, and this fragile earth, our island home. By your will they were created and have their being.

Addressing myriad environmental challenges requires us to move beyond the boundaries and safety of our churches and cathedrals to form and restore loving, liberating, and life-giving relationships with all of creation. This begins with growing our love for the earth and all of life.

It continues with standing alongside marginalized, vulnerable peoples, advocating and acting to repair creation, and seeking the liberation and flourishing of all people. And finally, it requires us to find practical ways of living humbly and gently with the earth. This includes reorienting our relationship with the material world and examining our consumption levels, modes of travel, and other interactions with the earth.

We do this not because God needs anything from us but rather to reflect God's love and justice. We are called to expand our boundary of care, approaching the natural world with the same compassion and love that God has shown us.

Delia R. Heck, PhD
Professor of Environmental Science, Science, and Technology
Division Chair, Ferrum College
Callaway, Virginia

Questions

In what ways is God calling you out of human-made shrines to address the environmental challenges facing our island home?

How might you stand alongside marginalized, vulnerable peoples as they seek liberation and flourishing?

What types of advocacy might you engage in to help repair creation?

How might you change your consumption levels or travel patterns to live more gently with the earth?

Prayer

O God, who made the world and everything in it and gives us life and breath and all things, help us to form and restore loving, liberating, life-giving relationships with all of creation through Jesus Christ our Lord. *Amen.*

Romans 8:18-23

[18]I consider that the sufferings of this present time are not worth comparing with the glory about to be revealed to us. [19]For the creation waits with eager longing for the revealing of the children of God; [20]for the creation was subjected to futility, not of its own will but by the will of the one who subjected it, in hope [21]that the creation itself will be set free from its bondage to decay and will obtain the freedom of the glory of the children of God. [22]We know that the whole creation has been groaning in labor pains until now; [23]and not only the creation, but we ourselves, who have the first fruits of the Spirit, groan inwardly while we wait for adoption, the redemption of our bodies.

Reflection

In many cultures, farmers traditionally set apart the first fruits as an offering to God. The gift demonstrates the understanding that everything belongs to God, and that we are the stewards of God's creation. The offering says, "the best is yet to come!"

We, those who believe, have become the first fruits of the Spirit. We have been set free from bondage and fear through our faith, and we live in anticipation of the goodness that is to come. However, our promise of future glory is not for ourselves alone.

The creation, which is inclusive of all of humankind, all life, and the earth, waits with us. We are awaiting the reconciliation between God and humankind and a return to a time of harmony with the earth. As the first fruits, we are different from the creation, not because we are separate or above, but because we understand this moment in a different way.

For others, suffering may simply be suffering. For us, hardship and suffering evoke the immediacy of birth pains. We experience the anticipation of something promised that will certainly be revealed. Others may have seen Jesus's death on the cross as finality, while we see the resurrection as hope for a new earth and a new heaven.

We have been set apart for the sole purpose of being an example for others. Our role now, in collaboration with God, is to become proactive in our stewardship of God's creation. We hold the responsibility of setting the creation free from bondage and death. Along with God, we can usher in hope and abundant life.

Dr. Gabrie'l J. Atchison
Missioner for Administration
Episcopal dioceses of Western New York
& Northwestern Pennsylvania
Kenmore, New York

Questions

Creation care contains a call for economic and racial justice in addition to a move to improve our connection with nature and the earth. What are some everyday actions we can take to bring us closer to a vision of reconciliation?

How does the analogy of adoption (verse 23) empower us as Christians in our efforts for greater inclusion in our lives and worship spaces?

Prayer

Our Creator, thank you for giving us ample opportunities to care for all of your creation, for we know that through caring for creation, we commune with you. Help us not only to have patience in suffering but also to help others understand the glory that will be revealed through this work. *Amen.*

Galatians 6:7-9

7Do not be deceived; God is not mocked, for you reap whatever you sow. 8If you sow to your own flesh, you will reap corruption from the flesh; but if you sow to the Spirit, you will reap eternal life from the Spirit. 9So let us not grow weary in doing what is right, for we will reap at harvesttime, if we do not give up.

Reflection

We all experience difficult times that test our faith. When this happens, we might be tempted to avoid doing the right thing by turning away from God, from the great fabric of life, and from our communities, neighbors, and friends. In these moments, we often tell ourselves: "What difference will it make?" On the surface, statements like that sound like a question, but with some discernment, we begin to realize that phrases like this help rationalize our temptation to give up or give in.

Standing firm in his faith, Saint Paul encourages us to meet our despair with clear-minded persistence and hope. Because his words are grounded in practical wisdom—we are part of God's creation—they remind us that our actions or lack of actions have consequences. For that reason, they point directly to the spiritual path that Jesus wants us to take.

The temptation to give up when we feel despair is as real in our day as it was 2,000 years ago, perhaps even more so given the ecological and climate emergency that we face. The way of Christ calls us not to ignore or deny the realities of this world, as difficult and overwhelming as they may be. Instead, Jesus wants us to keep our hearts and minds awake. He wants us to strengthen our resistance to the temptation of despair by never giving up on our faith and good works.

This makes Saint Paul's encouragement all the more direct and clearer. The seeds of loving-kindness and bold stewardship that we sow today will be harvested by generations to come. They will be God's gift from us to them, seeds spread by our faithful hearts, minds, and hands.

The Rev. Canon Jeff Golliher, PhD
Assisting Minister Provincial for Sacred Ecology, Society of Saint Francis, Third Order, Province of the Americas, and Missioner Ellenville, Diocese of New York

Questions

To follow in the way of Christ requires us to discern our habits of giving in to temptation so our lives will radiate true faith and hope. Can you remember discerning moments when you chose to stand firm in your faith and do the right thing?

Can you remember moments when friends helped you to discern?

Can you think of ways to sow seeds of good environmental stewardship and justice today?

Prayer

Gracious God, you are with us in every moment of our lives. We pray that you will help us awaken to the call that you have given to us—to care for a world that is not ours to plunder but a world that you placed in our care. Teach us to discern how we can weave together what we have torn apart, bringing the light of Christ to your world with thankfulness, humility, and joy. *Amen.*

Colossians 1:15-17

[15]He is the image of the invisible God, the firstborn of all creation; [16]for in him all things in heaven and on earth were created, things visible and invisible, whether thrones or dominions or rulers or powers—all things have been created through him and for him. [17]He himself is before all things, and in him all things hold together.

Reflection

Every living organism originated from a common ancestor; there is one DNA, and all plants and animals share it. The carbon, nitrogen, and oxygen in our bodies, in all animals and plants and in the earth itself, were created by generations of stars. Intuitively the apostle Paul knew it as did John when he wrote, "In the beginning was the Word…" (John 1:1). Cradled in the great forests of the world, the air that gives us life gives breath to fishes of the sea and everything that lives, and it has been so since the beginning some 4.6 billion years ago when a supernova in our galaxy, the Milky Way, exploded and a new star, our sun, was born. As swirling gasses and dust broke off from the sun, planets were created, including Earth and the moon. Discoveries in the 1990s revealed the extent of the observable universe from surveys taken by NASA's Hubble Space Telescope, and we have learned about the chemical composition of life on Earth through comparisons with moon rocks and meteorites.

As astronomer Carl Sagan reminds us, "We are a way for the universe to know itself. Some part of our bodies knows this is where we come from. We are star-stuff!" We are related to every human being of every culture, color, tongue, and land; we are related to all animals on earth, all fish, all plants, rocks, and rocky mountain ridges, and every star, moon, sun, and planet in the universe. In Christ, "the first-born of all creation," not some but all creation, was formed. In Christ, all things hold together. Notice the use of the word "all." We are all linked together, held in the loving embrace of God. There is a phrase in the Lakota language that expresses oneness with all, *Mitákuye oyás'in*, which is to say, all my relations: everyone and everything is related in the one glorious, magnificent web of life.

Anne Rowthorn, PhD
Episcopal lay leader and author
Salem, Connecticut

Questions _____

Where, when, and how do you find your deepest connection to God's good earth, and how do you nurture it?

Pope Francis has said that an "ecological conversion" is not an optional or a secondary experience of our lives as Christians. We all need an ecological conversion, both for our own well-being and, more essentially, the well-being of our precious planet. What do you think about this statement?

Prayer _____

Praise to you, holy God of the universe. You were there at the dawning of creation, and you hold all things together. You roll out the ever-expanding celestial tapestry of bright stars, bursting supernovas, spinning planets, and galaxies beyond galaxies, yet you are as near to us as the air we breathe. You hover close to the newborn, and you will soothe our dying breath. All praise to you, holy God, and thank you! *Amen.*

2 Timothy 1:6-14

⁶For this reason I remind you to rekindle the gift of God that is within you through the laying on of my hands; ⁷for God did not give us a spirit of cowardice, but rather a spirit of power and of love and of self-discipline. ⁸Do not be ashamed, then, of the testimony about our Lord or of me his prisoner, but join with me in suffering for the gospel, relying on the power of God, ⁹who saved us and called us with a holy calling, not according to our works but according to his own purpose and grace. This grace was given to us in Christ Jesus before the ages began, ¹⁰but it has now been revealed through the appearing of our Savior Christ Jesus, who abolished death and brought life and immortality to light through the gospel. ¹¹For this gospel I was appointed a herald and an apostle and a teacher, ¹²and for this reason I suffer as I do. But I am not ashamed, for I know the one in whom I have put my trust, and I am sure that he is able to guard until that day what I have entrusted to him. ¹³Hold to the standard of sound teaching that you have heard from me, in the faith and love that are in Christ Jesus. ¹⁴Guard the good treasure entrusted to you, with the help of the Holy Spirit living in us.

Reflection

As climate changes, we experience more frequent and intense heatwaves. Hotter, drier conditions lead to bigger and more damaging wildfires. Warmer oceans fuel bigger, stronger hurricanes and typhoons. Suffering multiplies as crops fail, and water becomes ever scarcer.

In light of these alarming changes, it's natural to feel sad and afraid, frustrated, or even hopeless. It's easy to be paralyzed by the magnitude of the problem and the relative insignificance of our actions.

As Christians, though, we have a litmus test for our response to such challenges. God has not given us a spirit of fear, the apostle Paul writes to Timothy. When we respond out of fear or we let that fear grow into anxiety or panic, or harden into denial, we know that response is not from God.

Instead, Paul reminds Timothy that God has given us three remarkable gifts. The first is *power*. Though power is an old-fashioned word, its meaning is still current: God empowers us. If we are empowered, we can act rather than be frozen or paralyzed by fear.

But that's not all. God has also given us *love*. In the Gospel of John, Jesus says, "By this everyone will know that you are my disciples, if you have love for one another" (John 13:35). We can and should be recognized by our ability to have compassion for others, care for others, and put their needs first—and the fact that we're able to do so is a gift from God.

Lastly, God has gifted us with a *sound mind*. We may not always choose to use it, but God has given us the ability to make good decisions based on facts and information. And when God makes those evident in his creation, that's what we call science.

Think of all the people and other living things already affected by climate change today. Caring about and acting to preserve God's creation is entirely consistent with the gifts God has given us. And we can do this powered by God's love and a sound mind.

Dr. Katharine Hayhoe
Paul Whitfield Horn Distinguished Professor and Endowed Chair in Public Policy and Public Law, Texas Tech University
Chief Scientist, The Nature Conservancy
Lubbock, Texas

Questions

What are some fears that climate change raises for you?

What is something specific you could do to act on climate in a way that demonstrates God's love?

What would it look like for the church to respond to climate change with power, love, and a sound mind?

Prayer

Gracious God, thank you for the gifts you have given us. Thank you for the calling we have received. Thank you that we are not judged according to our works but according to your purpose and grace as we walk in the good works you have prepared and equipped us for in advance. *Amen.*

Revelation 22:1-8

¹Then the angel showed me the river of the water of life, bright as crystal, flowing from the throne of God and of the Lamb ²through the middle of the street of the city. On either side of the river is the tree of life with its twelve kinds of fruit, producing its fruit each month; and the leaves of the tree are for the healing of the nations. ³Nothing accursed will be found there any more. But the throne of God and of the Lamb will be in it, and his servants will worship him; ⁴they will see his face, and his name will be on their foreheads. ⁵And there will be no more night; they need no light of lamp or sun, for the Lord God will be their light, and they will reign forever and ever.

⁶And he said to me, "These words are trustworthy and true, for the Lord, the God of the spirits of the prophets, has sent his angel to show his servants what must soon take place." ⁷"See, I am coming soon! Blessed is the one who keeps the words of the prophecy of this book." ⁸I, John, am the one who heard and saw these things. And when I heard and saw them, I fell down to worship at the feet of the angel who showed them to me.

Reflection

I've lived my entire life in cities. Like many urbanites—and like most people, as survey after survey shows—my most resonant experiences of God happen outdoors. A sublime sunrise. Mountains glistening in the day's brightness. The subtle bend of the arm of a tree on a city street. Repeatedly, divine depth and fullness of life reach me through the planet. "In wildness is the preservation of the world," wrote Henry David Thoreau more than a century ago, when modern industrial society was starting to plant its chokehold on the planet. I know exactly what he meant.

But in Revelation 22:2, we're reminded that the natural world has an additional power beyond resuscitating world-weary, solitary souls deprived of grace or devastated by poverty or addiction. "The leaves of the trees are for the healing of the nations," the text says. Nature, it turns out, doesn't just save people as individuals. It saves us as a collective—as "nations."

As the impact of climate change becomes increasingly clear—droughts and fires that drive people from their homes and homelands, and rising seas and severe storms that destroy long-established communities—this passage becomes more important. Nature's sacred power to heal us, whether individually or collectively, isn't infinite.

There is such a thing as too much abuse for God's creation. Scientists have been clear for decades that we have entered multiple environmental danger zones. Now, like it or not, we have reached a point of emergency. Those of us alive now—the collective of the present—must find our courage and act. We must protect the planet because it is sacred.

Our spiritual growth is always moral growth. It involves not only our becoming more alive but also more responsible for the well-being of all. So, the next time you hear about a climate change march or campaign, do a favor for the future and step up. Many have renewed their faith by participating in great social movements. There is none more important today than protecting our precious planet, our island home.

The Rev. Fletcher Harper
Executive Director of GreenFaith
Secaucus, New Jersey

Questions

Do you think of your faith as something individual or as involving people and planet collectively? Can you think of a time when your faith moved you to act for the good of all?

Have you ever participated in a social movement because your faith motivated you to do so? If yes, what was the experience like? If no, what blocks you from doing so?

Prayer

Dear God, you have given us the gift of life on your beautiful earth. We tremble now because we know that it is at risk. Give us new wisdom and courage to live out our faith in ways that we have not yet done, ways that show our conviction that people and planet together are sacred. When we are timid, embolden us. When we are frightened to lift our voices, help us find the right words and right spirit. And through these actions, draw us more deeply into the mystery of your love, in Jesus's Name. *Amen.*

Additional Biblical Texts about Creation Care

Old Testament Lessons

Genesis 1:9-10—God called the dry land Earth

Genesis 1:11-13—Let the earth put forth vegetation

Genesis 1:14-19—God made the two great lights

Genesis 1:20-23—Let the waters bring forth swarms of living creatures

Genesis 1:28-31—Be fruitful and multiply

Genesis 3:8-19—Cursed is the ground because of you

Genesis 6:5-8—I will blot out from the earth the human beings I have created

Genesis 6:18-20—I will establish my covenant with you

Genesis 7:1-16—Take with you seven pairs of all clean animals

Genesis 9:1-17—This is the sign of the covenant that I make between me and you and every living creature that is with you

Genesis 41:37-57—Seven years of famine began to come

Exodus 7:14-25—The fish in the river shall die, the river itself shall stink

Exodus 9:1-7—All the livestock of the Egyptians died

Exodus 9:13-35—Stretch out your hand toward heaven so that hail may fall on the whole land of Egypt

Exodus 10:1-20—The locusts came upon all the land of Egypt

Leviticus 24:18-21—Anyone who kills an animal shall make restitution for it, life for life

Leviticus 25:13-24—You shall observe my statutes and faithfully keep my ordinances, so that you may live on the land securely

Leviticus 26:3-6—If you follow my statutes and keep my commandments and observe them faithfully, I will give you your rains in their season

Leviticus 26:14-16, 32-35—I will devastate the land, so that your enemies who come to settle in it shall be appalled at it

Numbers 11:31-35—Then a wind went out from the Lord, and it brought quails from the sea and let them fall beside the camp

Numbers 20:1-13—Command the rock before their eyes to yield its water

Deuteronomy 6:10-19—The Lord your God has brought you into the land that he swore to your ancestors

Deuteronomy 7:12-13—God will love you, bless you, and multiply you

Deuteronomy 8:1-10—For the Lord your God is bringing you into a good land

Deuteronomy 11:1-17—Love the Lord your God and serve him with all your heart and with all your soul

Deuteronomy 14:22-29—Set apart a tithe of all the yield of your seed

Deuteronomy 20:19-20—You must not destroy its trees by wielding an ax

Deuteronomy 22:6-7—If you come on a bird's nest

Deuteronomy 24:17-22—When you reap your harvest in your field and forget a sheaf in the field, you shall not go back to get it

Deuteronomy 28: 1-14—Blessed shall be the fruit of your womb, the fruit of your ground, and the fruit of your livestock

Deuteronomy 28:15-46—But if you will not obey the Lord your God diligently observing all his commandments and decrees...

Deuteronomy 29:22-29—The next generation will see the devastation of that land and the afflictions with which the Lord has afflicted it

Joshua 5:13-15—The place where you stand is holy

Job 36:24-33—God distills his mist in rain

Job 37:1-18—Consider the wondrous works of God

Job 38:22-41—Who provides for the raven its prey?

Job 39:19-30—Is it by your wisdom that the hawk soars?

Psalm 46:1-11—There we will not fear

Psalm 48:1-14—Great is the Lord and greatly to be praised in the city of our God

Psalm 65:5-13—You visit the earth and water it

Psalm 74:12-17—You have fixed all the bounds of the earth

Psalm 78:35-55—He destroyed their vines with hail

Psalm 107:35-38—He turns rivers into a desert

Psalm 136:1-9—O give thanks to the Lord, for he is good

Psalm 146:5-9—Happy are those whose help is the God of Jacob

Psalm 147:1-17—God determines the number of the stars

Proverbs 8:22-36—Before the mountains had been shaped, before the hills, I was brought forth

Ecclesiastes 1:1-7—The earth remains forever

Song of Solomon 2:10-17—My beloved speaks

Song of Solomon 6:2-3, 11—My beloved has gone down to his garden

Isaiah 5:1-7—Let me sing for my beloved my love-song concerning his vineyard

Isaiah 11:6-8—The wolf shall live with the lamb

Isaiah 19:5-15—The waters of the Nile will be dried up

Isaiah 24:3-13, 19-20—The earth lies polluted under its inhabitants

Isaiah 30:23-26—He will give rain for the seed with which you sow the ground

Isaiah 41:17-20—I will open rivers on the bare heights

Jeremiah 12:4, 10-13—The whole land is made desolate

Jeremiah 46:22-23—They shall cut down her forest

Ezekiel 12:17-28—The inhabited cities shall be laid waste

Joel 1:15-2:5—Even the wild animals cry to you

Malachi 3:8-12—Will anyone rob God?

New Testament Lessons

Matthew 8:18-27—And when he got into the boat, his disciples followed him

Matthew 10:29-30—Are not two sparrows sold for a penny

Matthew 20:1-16—Parable of the Laborers in the Vineyard

Matthew 25:41-46—Lord, when was it that we saw you hungry or thirsty?

Matthew 26:26-30—Jesus took and broke bread

Mark 4:35-41—Jesus stills a storm

Mark 6:45-52—Jesus walks on water

Mark 9:2-3—Jesus went up the mountain

Luke 3:1-6—Prepare the way of the Lord

Luke 6:1-5—Jesus goes through the grain fields

Luke 9:10-17—Feeding of the five thousand

Luke 15:1-7—The Parable of the Lost Sheep

Luke 20:9-19—The Parable of the Wicked Tenants

Luke 21:29-33—Look at the fig tree and all the trees

John 1:1-18—In the beginning was the Word

John 4:1-30—Those who drink of the water that I will give them will never be thirsty.

John 6:22-51—I am the bread of life

John 10:1-18—I am the good shepherd

1 Corinthians 3:1-23—You are God's temple

1 Corinthians 10:23-11:1—Do not seek your own advantage, but that of the other

2 Corinthians 4:1-15—Treasure in clay jars

2 Corinthians 9:1-15—He who supplies seed to the sower and bread for food

Revelation 8:1:13—A third of the waters became wormwood

Revelation 11:11-19—Destroying those who destroy the earth

Revelation 21:1-8—A new heaven and new earth

Revelation 21:9-27—The vision of the new Jerusalem

The Creation Care Bible Challenge

Marc Andrus is the eighth bishop of the Episcopal Diocese of California. He has headed the presiding bishop's delegation to the United Nations climate summits, beginning with the 2015 summit that produced the Paris Agreement. He serves on the leaders circle of America Is All In, a coalition of cities, states, faith bodies, tribal nations, universities, and health systems working together to help the United States keep its commitment to the Paris Agreement and limit global warming. Marc also helps represent the Episcopal Church in the Anglican Communion Environmental Network. He is the co-author, with Matthew Fox, of *Stations of the Cosmic Christ*, which won two Nautilus Gold awards, and the author of the forthcoming book, *Brothers in the Beloved Community: The Friendship of Thich Nhat Hanh and Martin Luther King, Jr.* He is married to Sheila Andrus, and they have two adult daughters, Pilar and Chloé. *Day 3*

Jim Antal is the special advisor on climate justice to the general minister and president of the United Church of Christ. His book, *Climate Church, Climate World: How People of Faith Must Work for Change,* is being read by hundreds of congregations. Jim is a graduate of Princeton University, Yale Divinity School, and Andover Newton Theological School. He has preached on climate change since 1988 in more than 300 settings and has engaged in nonviolent civil disobedience many times. In 2018, he retired as the leader of the 350 United Church of Christ congregations in Massachusetts. He wrote three groundbreaking national United Church of Christ resolutions: in 2013 on divesting from fossil fuel companies; in 2017 to declare a new moral era to oppose withdrawal from the Paris Agreement; and in 2019 to endorse the Green New Deal. *Day 33*

Gabrie'l J. Atchison serves as the missioner for administration in the Episcopal dioceses of Western New York and Northwestern Pennsylvania. She holds a master of arts degree in religion from Yale Divinity School and received her doctorate in gender studies from Clark University. She is the editor of the Environment and Religion in Feminist-Womanist,

Queer, and Indigenous Perspectives Series for Lexington Books and the co-author of *More to This Confession: Relational Prison Theology. Day 46*

Harold W. Attridge is the Sterling Professor of Divinity, Emeritus, at Yale Divinity School. He also taught at Perkins School of Theology at Southern Methodist University, and the theology department at the University of Notre Dame. He was educated at Boston College, Cambridge, and Harvard. He served as dean of the faculty of Arts and Letters at Notre Dame (1991-1997) and dean of Yale Divinity School (2002-2012). He has made scholarly contributions to the study of Hellenistic Judaism, Gnostic literature, the Epistle to the Hebrews, and the Gospel of John. He was elected to the American Academy of Arts and Sciences in 2015. *Day 15*

Dave Bookless is an author, writer, eco-theologian, and Anglican parish priest. His doctorate from Cambridge University examines biblical approaches to the value of wildlife and ecosystems. He has spoken in more than 40 countries across six continents and written or contributed to more than 20 books, including *Planetwise*, translated into six languages. Alongside pastoring a small, multiracial church and his work for A Rocha (arocha.org), he is a Lausanne catalyst for creation care and serves on the Church of England's Environment Working Group. He is married to Anne, also ordained, and they have four adult daughters. He enjoys running, birding, and Indian food. *Day 6*

Margaret Bullitt-Jonas is an Episcopal priest, author, public speaker, and climate activist. She has been a lead organizer of many Christian and interfaith events about care for Earth. She offers retreats in the United States and Canada on spiritual resilience and resistance amid climate emergencies. She serves as missioner for creation care for the Episcopal Diocese of Western Massachusetts and the Southern New England Conference, United Church of Christ, and as creation care advisor for the Episcopal Diocese of Massachusetts. Her latest book, *Rooted and Rising: Voices of Courage in a Time of Climate Crisis* (2019), co-edited with Leah Schade, features essays by religious environmental activists with study questions and spiritual practices. She maintains a website at RevivingCreation.org. *Day 5*

Jenny Rose Carey is a renowned gardener, educator, and public speaker, and author of several gardening books, including *Glorious Shade: Dazzling Plants, Design Ideas, and Proven Techniques for Your Shady Garden*. She has served as the Temple University Director of the Ambler Arboretum and adjunct professor in the Department of Landscape Architecture and Horticulture and as the senior director at the Pennsylvania Horticultural Society's Meadowbrook Farm in Jenkintown, Pennsylvania. She lives and gardens at Northview, her Victorian property in Pennsylvania, but grew up in the countryside in Kent, England, where her botanist father was also a lay minister. She has spent much of her life encouraging others to get out into nature and start their own gardens. Jenny Rose grew up in the Church of England but is now a member of the Episcopal Church. *Day 25*

Tom Chappell was baptized at St. Paul's in Wickford, Rhode Island, sang as a choirboy at St. Stephen's in Pittsfield, Massachusetts, and served as an acolyte at Trinity Church, Whitinsville, Massachusetts. He is currently a member of St. David's Episcopal Church, Kennebunk, Maine. He graduated from the Moses Brown School and earned a degree in English at Trinity College and a master of theological studies degree at Harvard Divinity School. He is co-founder of Tom's of Maine, a pioneer in natural personal care products sold to Colgate-Palmolive. He is also a co-founder of Ramblers Way Farm, Inc., a pioneer in certified organic merino clothing. Tom is married to Kate Cheney Chappell, artist, sculptor, and poet. They are parents of five children and have 10 grandchildren. They live in Kennebunk, Maine, and Monhegan Island, Maine. *Day 42*

Shaun Cozett is the rector of St. Paul's Bree Street in the Anglican Diocese of Cape Town in South Africa, where he also serves as the coordinator of the Diocesan Environment Resource Team. He is a founding member of the Southern African Faith Communities' Environment Institute and currently serves on the board of directors. Before pursuing ordination, he worked as a partnership coordinator in the National Government's

Environmental Programs, implementing various projects to create jobs through the management of invasive alien plants; his work includes the award-winning eco-coffins project. He is currently a post-graduate student in environmental humanities at the University of Cape Town. *Day 36*

Jenny Te Paa Daniel (Te Rarawa) is Te Mareikura (the esteemed indigenous professor) at the National Centre for Peace and Conflict Studies, Otago University, Dunedin. Previously she served for 23 years as Te Ahorangi (the principal) at St. John's Anglican Theological College in Auckland, New Zealand. During her lengthy tenure, she established herself as one of a small group of leading Anglican women theological writers and teachers. Highly respected globally and nationally for her fearlessness in critiquing injustice and for her relentless advocacy for women's leadership, she has been awarded five international honorary doctorates and two prestigious distinguished alumni awards in recognition of her leadership example and her prolific scholarship. Jenny lives in both Aitutaki and Auckland, enjoying a balanced lifestyle, which prioritizes affinity with and affection for *whanau* (family), *whenua* (the land), and *moana* (the ocean). *Day 35*

C. Andrew "Andy" Doyle serves as the bishop of the Episcopal Diocese of Texas. He is a visionary leader, teacher, and author. His latest book is *Embodied Liturgy: Virtual Reality and Liturgical Theology in Conversation*. His initiatives include mission and church planting, leadership through the divisions on sexuality, memorializing the 1979 Book of Common Prayer while sustaining liturgical innovation, and racial reparations and justice. Today he is curious about global voices on environmental leadership. He is an outdoor enthusiast and fly fisher. *Day 1*

Manuel Ernesto is the bishop of the Anglican Diocese of Nampula in Mozambique. He is the liaison bishop for the environment in the Anglican Church of Southern Africa. Over the last ten years, he has worked with the refugee communities, mainly from Eastern Africa's Great Lakes region, Burundi, Rwanda, the Democratic Republic of Congo, South Sudan, and Somalia. Since 2017, the refugee and migration pastorate in the Diocese of Nampula has expanded to include the internally displaced people who flee from Islamist extremism in the gas and oil fields of Cabo Delgado, along the border with Tanzania. *Day 10*

Rachel Field lives on a hillside in the Green Mountains, the ancestral homeland of the Abenaki people, amid a vast collection of mosses, flowers, mushrooms, warblers, microbes, and mammals, with her husband, Jonathan, and their livestock. Together they care for and are cared for by a community of chickens, cows, horses, pigs, ducks, guinea hens, and goats on their home farm called Heartberry Hollow Farm and Forest. Rachel is an Episcopal priest and farmer who enjoys making up short rhymes about plants and singing them to her horse Tom Bombadil, because he never complains about them. When not outside, she is most likely curled up reading Tolkien or C.S. Lewis with her cat, Eowyn. *Day 32*

Elizabeth Garnsey was ordained in the Episcopal Diocese of New York in 2006 after a career in journalism. She currently serves as associate rector at St. Mark's Episcopal Church in New Canaan, Connecticut, where she lives with her eight-year-old son. She holds a certificate in conservation and environmental sustainability from Columbia University's Earth Institute. *Day 7*

Jeff Golliher is assisting minister provincial for sacred ecology in the Anglican Society of St. Francis, Third Order, and missioner for the Episcopal Diocese of New York, where he also serves at St. John's Episcopal Church, Ellenville. He has previously worked as canon for the environment at the Cathedral of St. John the Divine in Manhattan and at the Office of the Anglican Communion at the United Nations. Before ordination to the priesthood, he received a doctorate in cultural anthropology. He has authored and edited several books on Christian spirituality and faith responses to the environmental and climate crisis. He is married to Lynne "Asha" Golliher. *Day 47*

Karenna Gore is the founder and executive director of the Center for Earth Ethics (CEE) at Union Theological Seminary. CEE bridges the worlds of religion, academia, activism, and policymaking to discern and pursue the changes in policy and culture necessary to create a value system based on the long-term health of the whole. She is an *ex officio* member of the faculty of the Earth Institute at Columbia University. Karenna has worked as a lawyer, a nonprofit administrator, and a writer and is the author of *Lighting the Way: Nine Women Who Changed Modern America*. She grew up between middle Tennessee and northern Virginia and now lives in New York City with her three children. She is the daughter of Al and Tipper Gore. *Day 24*

Jerusalem Jackson Greer is a writer and speaker and serves as the staff officer for evangelism in the Office of the Presiding Bishop in the Episcopal Church. Part of her job is shepherding the Good News Gardens initiative, a church-wide movement of food and creation care ministries. Jerusalem has authored two books, *A Homemade Year: The Blessings of Cooking, Crafting, and Coming Together* (based on the liturgical calendar), *At Home in this Life: Finding Peace at the Crossroads of Unraveled Dreams and Beautiful Surprises* (based on the Rule of Saint Benedict), and a host of faith curricula. She lives with her family on a hobby farm in Central Arkansas. You can learn more about her at jerusalemgreer.com. *Day 28*

Eliza Griswold is a poet and journalist who writes about systems and interconnectedness. Her most recent book, *If Men, Then: Poems*, explores the final age of humankind. Eliza spent seven years in Appalachia with families affected by fracking who were attempting to fight against their erasure from land where they had lived for more than a century. Her book *Amity and Prosperity: One Family and the Fracturing of America* was awarded the 2019 Pulitzer Prize. *Day 13*

Fletcher Harper serves as executive director of GreenFaith. After serving as a parish priest for a decade, he became a pioneer of the global religious environmental movement, leading GreenFaith from its early life as a New Jersey-focused, multi-faith group to its current work as an international, interfaith, climate justice organization. He has helped spearhead the faith-based fossil fuel divestment movement and organized hundreds of thousands of people to participate in major climate mobilizations. He is a co-founder of Shine, an international campaign that supports women-

and community-led renewable energy access initiatives in Africa and India and helped launch the Interfaith Rainforest Initiative. He is the author of *GreenFaith: Mobilizing God's People to Protect the Earth. Day 50*

Katharine Hayhoe is an atmospheric scientist who studies climate change, one of the most pressing issues facing humanity today. She may be best-known to many for her efforts to call Christians to climate action and to bridge the broad, deep gap between scientists and people of faith. She is the chief scientist for The Nature Conservancy and a distinguished professor and chair at Texas Tech University. Katharine also serves as the World Evangelical Alliance's climate ambassador and science advisor to the Evangelical Environmental Network, Young Evangelicals for Climate Action, and A Rocha USA. She hosts the PBS Digital Series *Global Weirding* and is the author of *Saving Us: A Climate Scientist's Case for Hope and Healing in a Divided World. Day 49*

Delia R. Heck is a professor of environmental science and chair of the sciences and technology division at Ferrum College, where she has been teaching since 1998. Her research focuses on environmental and climate justice. She is also the director of the Smith Mountain Lake Water Quality Monitoring Program. She is a member of the Episcopal Church's Taskforce on Care of Creation, where she leads the working group on environmental racism. She holds doctorate and master of science degrees in geography from the University of Washington and a bachelor of science in regional development from the University of Arizona. She has been married to the Rev. John H. Heck for 24 years. They have two sons and one grandson. *Day 45*

Margot R. Hodson is director of theology and education at the John Ray Initiative, an educational charity that combines science, the environment, and the Christian faith for sustainability and action. She teaches environmental theology and rural ministry at Ripon College, Cuddesdon, Oxford, United Kingdom. Currently serving as a priest in the English Cotswolds, she has previously been chaplain of Jesus College, Oxford. Margot has been passionate about environmental issues since her teens and sees this as an integral part of her Christian faith and ministry. She speaks and writes widely on these issues, and her latest publications include *Green Reflections: Biblical Inspiration for Sustainable Living*, written with her husband, Martin J. Hodson. *Day 19*

Martin J. Hodson is a plant scientist, environmental biologist, former principal lecturer, and now visiting researcher at Oxford Brookes University. He is also an associate member of the Institute of Human Sciences at the University of Oxford. He has served for 13 years as operations director for the John Ray Initiative. Martin is also principal tutor of Christian Rural and Environmental Studies (CRES), a distance-learning course. He writes and speaks widely on environmental issues and has over 100 publications, mostly in international science journals. His most recent book, with Margot Hodson, is the second edition of *A Christian Guide to Environmental Issues*. *Day 30*

Stephanie Johnson serves as the rector of St. Paul's Episcopal Church in Riverside, Connecticut. She has worked as an environmental planner and educator in government and corporate settings for 20 years. Following her ordination in the Episcopal Church, she worked for the New England bishops, leading congregational greening programs. She offers workshops and retreats on eco-theology, preaching on climate change and congregational greening. She is the chair of the Episcopal Church's Task Force on the Care of Creation and Environmental Racism. She also serves on the Leadership Council of Blessed Tomorrow and the Advisory Board of the Center for Earth Ethics. She is the author of *How Can I Care for Creation? A Little Book of Guidance* and co-author of the curriculum *A Life of Grace for the Whole World: A Study Course on the House of Bishops' Pastoral Teaching on the Environment*. *Day 44*

Mike Kinman is a follower of Jesus, spouse, parent, friend and rector of All Saints Church in Pasadena, California. He is a member of the Global Advisory Council of Thistle Farms, working with women survivors of trafficking, prostitution and addiction around the globe building communities of healing, love and economic justice. He is the former dean of Christ Church Cathedral in St. Louis and former executive director of Episcopalians for Global Reconciliation, which helped focus the church on the work of ending extreme poverty and addressing crucial global issues of environmental sustainability. *Day 12*

Nicholas Knisely is the thirteenth bishop of the Episcopal Diocese of Rhode Island. He studied physics and astronomy before attending seminary. For more than twenty years, he has taught and written on the intersection of faith and science. As a priest, he led spiritual outings and outdoor adventure retreats. As bishop, he has participated in the Connecticut River Pilgrimage and designed and co-led the Wood River Pilgrimage. The diocese he serves is installing a large solar power facility that will provide discounted renewable energy to nonprofits in the state. *Day 18*

Bill Lupfer has been a parish priest for three decades. He is currently serving as priest-in-charge at Christ Church, Aspen, Colorado, and formerly served as rector of Trinity Church, Wall Street. Bill met God doing a three-day solo on the Missinabai River in Canada and has marveled at all aspects of God's creation ever since. He learned much about creation care from his grandfather, a physician farmer, who understood the benefits of rot and decay long before recycling became popular. His wife, Kimiko, and her family in Japan, continue to teach him about caring for God's creation: smart house, limited electrical use, extensive recycling. Good friends in India show him how to use table scraps to fertilize their extensive garden while, at the same time, providing methane gas for cooking. *Day 29*

Rachel Mash is the environmental coordinator of the Anglican Church of Southern Africa, which includes South Africa, Eswatini, Lesotho, Namibia, Angola, and Mozambique. She is the secretary of the Anglican Communion Environmental Network and a member of the steering committee of the Ecumenical Season of Creation movement. She received a Lambeth award of the Order of St. Augustine for her services to the Anglican Communion in environmental ministry. *Day 8*

Gregory Mobley is an American Baptist minister and professor of Hebrew Bible at Yale Divinity School. Mobley came to Yale in 2017 after twenty years of teaching Old Testament/Hebrew Bible at Andover Newton Theological School (1997-2017) and Union Theological Seminary in New York (1996-97). He is the author of three books, including *The Return of the Chaos Monsters—and Other Backstories of the Bible*, and co-edited the award-winning anthology of essays on interfaith learning, *My Neighbor's Faith: Stories of Interfaith Encounter, Growth, and Transformation*. Mobley has done archaeological fieldwork in Israel and served as an editorial assistant on the Dead Sea Scrolls project. *Days 26, 41*

Kate Moorehead is the tenth dean of St. John's Cathedral in Jacksonville, Florida. She is the mother of three boys and the author of seven books. Her second book, *Organic God: Lenten Meditations on the Words of Jesus*, was written to unpack the magnificent meaning behind the many images that Jesus uses from nature in his parables and teachings. Her eighth book, published by Forward Movement, will explore the vital signs of the spiritual life. St. John's Cathedral is launching JaxLab, a University of Florida master's degree program in architecture, sustainability, historic preservation, and hydro-generated urbanism. The program will be housed on the cathedral campus and address the needs of the downtown. Kate is also the vice-chair of Cathedral District-Jax, a nonprofit corporation designed to revitalize the urban core. In 2019, they planted 60 trees in the neighborhood. *Day 4*

Jacynthia Murphy is the operations support manager serving in the General Synod Office of the Anglican Church in Aotearoa, New Zealand and Polynesia and the Māori Council of Churches. She works with the Anglican Indigenous Network, Anglican Communion Environmental Network, Social Justice Unit for the Environment, Climate Resilience and Rapid Response, and Impact Investment and Divestment. She recently contributed to the "Prophetic Indigenous Voices on the Planetary Crisis" webinars. She is passionate about curbing the human detriment of creation that causes devastating impacts on indigenous practices and sustainability. *Day 14*

Te Kitohi Pikaahu is the Anglican Bishop of Tai Tokerau in the northern region of New Zealand. He was consecrated a bishop in 2002. He has been the chair of the Anglican Indigenous Network of the Anglican Communion since 2015. He had served on the International Anglican Liturgical Consultation since 2007 and is a member of the Liturgical Society, *Societas Liturgica*. He was ordained deacon in 1987 and a priest the following year. He graduated with a licentiate in theology from St. John's College, Auckland, New Zealand, in 1986, and with a master of theology degree from Westminster College, Oxford, in 1997. Bishop Pikaahu spent 15 years in various positions in Auckland, serving as the archdeacon of Tamaki Makaurau (Auckland) from 1997-2001. *Day 39*

Nicholas T. Porter is the founding director of Jerusalem Peacebuilders, a ministry of interfaith reconciliation that partners with Jewish, Christian, Muslim, and Druze institutions to provide educators and youth with the skills, relationships, and support they need to become effective leaders and change agents. An Episcopal priest and educator, Canon Porter served at St. George's Cathedral in Jerusalem, the American Cathedral in Paris (France), Emmanuel Church in Geneva (Switzerland), Trinity Church in Southport (Connecticut), and St. Mary's in the Mountains in Wilmington (Vermont). While on the board of the Berkeley Divinity School at Yale, Nicholas initiated strategic projects in mission and environmental theology. *Day 37*

James Prosek is an artist, writer, and naturalist born and raised in Easton, Connecticut. He has traveled the world to document the beauty and diversity of our lands and waterways. He is the author of more than a dozen books and has exhibited his work globally at museums such as the Yale University Art Gallery and the Royal Academy of the Arts in London. His first book was published while an undergraduate student at Yale, *Trout: An Illustrated History*, which earned him the title of the "Audubon of Fish." He has traveled and fished around the world and is known to fly fishermen around the globe. He has also written for the *New York Times* and *National Geographic*. *Day 43*

Rob Radtke is President & CEO of Episcopal Relief & Development, a post he has held since 2005. Among the organization's priorities is addressing the impact of a changing climate on the most vulnerable around the world. As part of Episcopal Relief & Development's commitment to creation care, it aims to be carbon neutral in 2022. *Day 11*

Anne Rowthorn is a spouse, mother, and grandmother. She has degrees from Columbia University (master of science) and New York University (doctorate). She has taught at all levels from elementary and high school to graduate school and worked as a community organizer, a professional interviewer, and a special projects writer for the Episcopal Church. Anne has written or compiled 13 books, specializing of late in the area of religion and ecology. Among her books are *Earth and All the Stars: Reconnecting with Nature through Hymns, Stories, Poems, and Prayers from the World's Great Religions and Cultures*; *Feast of the Universe: An Interfaith Sourcebook of Ecological Spirituality from the World's Cultures and Religions;* and *The Wisdom of John Muir: 100+ Selections from the Letters, Journals, and Essays of the Great Naturalist.* With her husband, Bishop Jeffery Rowthorn, she compiled the award-winning book *God's Good Earth: Praise and Prayer for Creation.* She has established two community gardens. Anne and Jeffery renew and refresh themselves daily on forest hiking trails. *Day 48*

Jeffery Rowthorn came from Union Theological Seminary in 1973 to Yale as one of three founding faculty members of the new Institute of Sacred Music. For the next fourteen years, he taught liturgy and served as Yale Divinity School's first chapel minister. In 1987, he was elected suffragan bishop of Connecticut, and then from 1994 to 2001, he served as bishop of the Episcopal congregations in Europe. During the past forty years, he has compiled three hymnals and written hymns, the best-known being "Lord, You Give the Great Commission." In 2018, he and his wife, Anne Rowthorn, published *God's Good Earth: Praise and Prayer for Creation. Day 21*

Anita Louise Schell is a native of Lancaster, Pennsylvania, and has served congregations and schools in New York City, Philadelphia, Vermont, and Rhode Island. She is the provisional priest-in-charge of St. Ann's, Old Lyme,

Connecticut. She holds degrees in music, English literature, and world religions from Brown University, General Theological Seminary, and the Episcopal Divinity School, where she wrote her doctoral thesis on the topic of environmental justice. She served as president of Rhode Island Interfaith Power & Light. She is a board director for the Swan Point Cemetery in Providence, Rhode Island, and is convener of the Environmental Network of the Episcopal Church in Connecticut. She is a member of the Alumni Executive Committee of the General Theological Seminary. *Day 2*

Jay Sidebotham serves as associate for formation at St. James' Episcopal Church in New York City. He also serves as senior consultant for RenewalWorks, a ministry of Forward Movement. He is growing in his understanding of the connection between discipleship and creation care. *Day 17*

Matthew Sleeth is the co-founder of Blessed Earth, a nonprofit that encourages biblical stewardship of all creation. He is the author of the introduction to *The Green Bible* and books such as *Reforesting Faith: What Trees Teach Us About the Nature of God and His Love for Us. Day 38*

Jane L. Snowdon has devoted more than thirty years to a career in scientific and applied informatics roles at the IBM T. J. Watson Research Center and IBM Watson Health. She is currently the deputy chief science officer for Scientific Operations at IBM Watson Health. She has conducted research in genomics, clinical trial data management systems, health care coordination and management, population health, and thermal models for energy-efficient buildings. As a member of Christ Church Greenwich's Grants and Outreach committees for more than five years, she has led monthly dinners at Inspirica's women's and Pacific House's men's shelters. She participated in New York City's CoolRoofs program to cover roofs with a white reflective coating, lowering buildings' internal temperatures. She received her PhD from the Georgia Institute of Technology, M.S. from the University of Michigan, and B.S. from Pennsylvania State University, all in industrial engineering. *Day 23*

Stephanie Spellers serves as a canon to Presiding Bishop Michael B. Curry and spearheads Episcopal efforts around evangelism, reconciliation, and creation care. Her newest book, *The Church Cracked Open: Disruption, Decline and New Hope for Beloved Community* (March 2021), follows on her popular titles *Radical Welcome: Embracing God, The Other and the Spirit of Transformation* and *The Episcopal Way*. Spellers has served as chaplain to the Episcopal House of Bishops, directed and taught mission and evangelism at General Theological Seminary, and served as a canon in the Diocese of Long Island. She founded The Crossing, a groundbreaking church within St. Paul's Cathedral in Boston, and has led numerous church-wide renewal and justice efforts. *Day 40*

Becca Stevens is a speaker, social entrepreneur, author, priest, founder of 10 justice initiatives, and president of Thistle Farms. She has been featured on PBS NewsHour, The Today Show, CNN, ABC World News, named a CNN Hero, and White House Champion of Change. Drawn from 25 years of leadership in mission-driven work, Becca leads important conversations across the country with an inspiring message that love is the strongest force for change in the world. *Day 34*

Andrew Sumani holds a master's degree in theological studies from Nashotah Seminary and is passionate about environmental issues. He initiated an environmental desk in the Diocese of Lake Malawi and served as the first diocesan environmental coordinator. He was also among the pioneer group that established the Malawi Creation Care Network. He is a FLEAT (Faith Leaders Environmental Advocacy Training) member of the South African Faith Communities Environment Institute, a South African-based organization. Last year, he contributed a creation care sermon to a book entitled *40 Devotions on Creation*. *Day 16*

Richelle Thompson serves as managing editor of Forward Movement and is a former journalist. She has contributed to several books and has written for *Forward Day by Day*. She and her husband, the Rev. Jeff Queen, have two children and live in the beautiful Bluegrass State, Kentucky. *Day 9*

Masango Roderick Warakula is a lecturer at the National Anglican Theological College of Zimbabwe (better known as Bishop Gaul College), where he teaches eco-theology and Old Testament studies. Ordained in 2012, he has served in various parishes in the Diocese of Harare, Zimbabwe. He is one of the precursors of the Green Churches Movement in Zimbabwe and worked in the diocesan environmental desk. He is a fellow and consultant for Green Faith International Network. His academic qualifications include a master's degree in international relations from Bindura University of Science Education and a diploma in Sustainable, Inclusive and Climate Resilient Cities Program from Lund University in Sweden. *Day 27*

Malcolm Clemens Young is the dean of Grace Cathedral in San Francisco, California, and the author of *The Spiritual Journal of Henry David Thoreau* and *The Invisible Hand in the Wilderness: Economics, Ecology and God*. He received his doctoral degree in theology from Harvard University and loves surfing in California and Maui. *Day 20*

Marek P. Zabriskie serves as rector of Christ Church in Greenwich, Connecticut, and has served churches in Tennessee, Virginia, and Pennsylvania. He is the founder and director of The Bible Challenge and the Center for Biblical Studies (thecenterforbiblicalstudies.org), which freely promotes and shares The Bible Challenge around the world. Over a million Anglicans have participated in it. He has hiked more than 1,500 miles across Spain and is an honorary canon at the Anglican Cathedral of the Redeemer in Madrid. He has edited ten books in The Bible Challenge series and authored *Doing the Bible Better: The Bible Challenge and the Transformation of the Episcopal Church. Days 22, 31*

ABOUT FORWARD MOVEMENT

Forward Movement is committed to inspiring disciples and empowering evangelists. We live out our ministry through publishing books, daily reflections, studies for small groups, and online resources.

More than a half-million people read our daily devotions through *Forward Day by Day*, which is also available in Spanish (*Adelante día a día*) and Braille, online, as a podcast, and as an app for your smartphones or tablets. We actively seek partners across the church and look for ways to provide resources that inspire and challenge.

A ministry of the Episcopal Church since 1935, Forward Movement is a nonprofit organization funded by sales of resources and gifts from generous donors. To learn more, visit forwardmovement.org